The Soldier's Return.

FRONTISPIECE. Life in the Army.

LIFE IN THE ARMY,

IN THE

DEPARTMENTS OF VIRGINIA, AND THE GULF,

INCLUDING

OBSERVATIONS IN NEW ORLEANS,

WITH AN

ACCOUNT OF THE AUTHOR'S LIFE AND EXPERIENCE IN THE MINISTRY.

BY
REV. J. CHANDLER GREGG,
OF THE
PHILADELPHIA ANNUAL CONFERENCE.

SECOND EDITION,
REVISED AND CORRECTED.

PHILADELPHIA:
PERKINPINE & HIGGINS,
No. 56 NORTH FOURTH STREET.
1868.

WESTCOTT & THOMSON, STEREOTYPERS.

TO

THE OFFICERS AND MEN

OF THE 127th REGIMENT, P. V.,

AND ALL THE BRAVE DEFENDERS OF OUR NATION,

WHO, RALLYING ROUND THEIR COUNTRY'S FLAG,

HAVE VINDICATED ITS HONOR, AND SECURED FOR THEIR POSTERITY

The Birthright of Liberty, Union, and Peace;

TO THE MEMORY

OF THE MULTITUDE OF WORTHY PATRIOTS,

WHO HAVE SACRIFICED THEIR LIVES UPON FREEDOM'S ALTAR;

AND TO

MY FELLOW-LABORERS IN THE GOSPEL,

WHOSE FRIENDSHIP I CHERISH,

THIS WORK

IS AFFECTIONATELY DEDICATED,

BY THE AUTHOR.

PREFACE.

THE reader, may desire to know the why, and wherefore of this publication. It is due that I should briefly meet, and satisfy such an inquiry.

When appointed Chaplain to the St. James' Army Hospital in New Orleans, La. I beguiled an occasional hour of loneliness, by jotting down some observations of men and things, which to me appeared novel, and worthy of note. To this I added, as time allowed, the reminiscences of my experience in the Army of the Potomac, during the stirring period I was in active service, with my recollections of great battles, and brave men. I then, to give a degree of completeness to this memoranda, tried to recall the scenes of my early youth, my conversion to God, entrance into the ministry, and the events of several active years, on various fields of labor, within the bounds of the Philadelphia Annual Conference.

On my return from the Department of the Gulf, and after being honorably mustered out of the service of my country, I occupied a short respite from duty in arranging the desultory material thus collected, and now yield to the request of my friends in giving my manuscript to the public, in the form of a book. It is simply a record of facts, experience, and observations, without pretension to literary excellence or merit; and hastily prepared, without the advantage of diary, journal, or access to sources from which, a more extended, and accurate production might have been compiled. My volume will merely claim an humble place among the many which have been the offspring of the great rebellion, and will stand as a memorial of many events, connected with the gallant Regiment, with which I had the honor to serve, and with my own personal history. To my friends, I hope its perusal will be a source of pleasure and profit, and to all into whose hands it may fall, a means of some good.

J. C. GREGG.

PHILADELPHIA, *February* 22d, 1866.

CONTENTS.

I.—AUTOBIOGRAPHY.

CHAPTER I.

BOYHOOD.

CHAPTER II.

CONVERSION.

CHAPTER III.

PREACHING.

CHAPTER IV.

THE ITINERANCY.

CHAPTER V.

CHURCH BUILDING.

CHAPTER VI.

ORDINATION.

CHAPTER VII.

LOYALTY.

CHAPTER VIII.

PERSONAL.

II.—ARMY OF THE POTOMAC.

CHAPTER IX.

MUSTERING.

CHAPTER X.

WAR.

CHAPTER XI.

WINTER IN CAMP.

CHAPTER XII.

HOOKER'S CAMPAIGN.

CHAPTER XIII.

THE ONE HUNDRED AND TWENTY-SEVENTH PENN'A VOLUNTEERS.

CHAPTER XIV.

NOTES OF TRAVEL.

III.—OBSERVATIONS IN NEW ORLEANS.

CHAPTER XV.

NEW ORLEANS.

CHAPTER XVI.

OBSERVATIONS CONTINUED.

CHAPTER XVII.

OBSERVATIONS CONTINUED.

CHAPTER XVIII.

OBSERVATIONS CONTINUED.

CHAPTER XIX.

OBSERVATIONS CONTINUED.

CHAPTER XX.

OBSERVATIONS CONTINUED.

CHAPTER XXI.

OBSERVATIONS CONTINUED.

CHAPTER XXII.

OBSERVATIONS CONTINUED.

CHAPTER XXIII.

OBSERVATIONS CONTINUED.

CHAPTER XXIV.

OBSERVATIONS CONTINUED.

CHAPTER XXV.

OBSERVATIONS CONTINUED.

CHAPTER XXVI.

OBSERVATIONS CONTINUED.

IV.—CONCLUSION.

CHAPTER XXX.

CONCLUSION.

LIFE IN THE ARMY.

AUTOBIOGRAPHY.

CHAPTER I.

BOYHOOD.

BIRTH-PLACE—REGION OF THE ALLEGHANIES—WILD BEASTS OF THE FOREST—VARIOUS KINDS OF REPTILES—THE RATTLE-SNAKE—MODE OF CAPTURE—GOOD FOR FOOD WHEN SMOKE-DRIED—GREAT BATTLE WITH SNAKES—VICTORY—FARMING WORK—TRAVEL IN THE MOUNTAINS—EDUCATION UNDER DIFFICULTIES—DUTY TO PARENTS—MY FATHER, THOMAS GREGG, AN INVENTIVE GENIUS—IRON MANUFACTURE—FIRST CUT NAILS—ACCOUNT OF THE FIRST IRON-CLAD MONITOR—THE TRUE INVENTOR—REVERSES IN FORTUNE—THE "ROCK OF FAITH"—CONVERSION—EXPERIENCE—A PRAYING MOTHER—ON THE VERGE OF JORDAN.

I WAS born in Fayette County, Western Pennsylvania, within the wild ranges of the Alleghany mountains, where the howl of the wolf, the scream of the panther, the cry of the catamount, the barking of the fox, the hooting of the owl, and the wail of the wild cat, formed a medley of music, which, during the first years of my life, was most familiar to my ears. My boyhood's days were spent in friendly companionship with pet bears, and familiarity with foxes, racoons, ground hogs, opossums, rabbits, and squirrels. Besides this array of animals, my investigations led me into close proximity with numerous classes of dangerous reptiles.

Among the number, whose distinguishing characteristics, I might name, were, the Black Snake, the Rattle-snake, and the Copperhead.

The Black Snake was found often from ten to twelve feet in length, with a white ring round the neck: this species, were called *racers* on account of their great speed. They are said to possess the power to charm young children, birds, and small animals; yet they were not generally regarded as a very dangerous enemy.

The Rattle-snake was found in that region, in large numbers. They were about three feet in length, and sometimes as thick as a man's arm. They were considered very poisonous: but from the fact that they usually give an alarm with their rattles, when about to strike, you can be aware of their presence, and may keep clear of danger. I have frequently assisted in capturing the Rattle-snake, by placing a forked stick over its neck, and then quickly cutting off the head. In this manner the reptile so shunned and dreaded, may be turned to some advantage, and I can testify that when well smoked, and cured, it is equal to smoked beef, and may be eaten, as tender, palatable, and wholesome food.

There were also to be found great dens of the *Copper-head Snake*, and this species were considered the most *poisonous*, *deceptive*, *dangerous* and mean of all the snake family. And, strange to say, after exploring many portions of the Alleghany mountains I never found one friend of the Copperhead—their presence was dreaded by both man and beast. I remember, while a boy, having a great pitched battle with a battalion of them, and after a closely-contested engagement, gaining a complete victory—by killing them all. I might have captured a few of them as prisoners of war, but, being so well acquainted with their wicked and deceptive nature, I considered it a very dangerous experiment.

My chief occupation was working on the farm from the age of eight years until I was seventeen. I took my lessons in planting corn, ploughing and harrowing among the rocks; manufacturing sugar, cider, apple butter and sour krout; felling trees, splitting rails, &c., &c. During this period of time I crossed the great Alleghany mountains seventeen times, a distance of one hundred and twenty miles. I had some regard to the fifth commandment, and did all in my power to honor and serve my aged parents. The great amount of healthy out-door exercise I was of necessity compelled to take, served a good purpose, in securing me a robust constitution and preventing me from becoming a dyspeptic.

My early educational advantages were few and far between; for, during my boyhood, I was only permitted to attend school a few weeks during the winter season of the year, and even then, not more than three days out of the week. With the care of the family and farm, to a great extent resting on my young shoulders, the snow often a foot to two feet deep, and the school-house several miles distant, my reader will perceive that my pursuit of knowledge was under difficulties.

The amount of education I have been enabled to acquire, has been in the hard school of adversity; for, while other boys and young men of my acquaintance were enabled to attend school regularly, and graduate at some college, I was compelled by a sense of duty, and the force of circumstances, to spend my time in laboring to maintain my parents, of whom, I deem it just and proper at this point to introduce a short sketch.

My father, Thomas Gregg, was born in New Castle County, Delaware, near the City of Wilmington. His father and grandfather were members of the Society of Friends, and he being brought up a strict Quaker, was also a member of that persuasion. While yet a young man, after writing five years for the Court at New Castle, he removed from his native state to Western Pennsylvania, where he engaged in the manufacture of cut nails; he being the first person who had produced this article in the west.

The nails he made commanded twenty-five cents per pound. This was about the year 1802.

He also turned his attention to making salt, but devoted himself chiefly to iron manufacture, and invented the first furnace ever used for smelting ore by the use of

Anthracite coal. Had he obtained a patent for this important discovery, it would have resulted in immense advantage to him pecuniarily.

But while absent in Delaware, his foreman, who had been left in charge of the works, to test thoroughly the invention, made a clean sweep of all his papers, patterns, and drawings, and fled to England, where he, and others speedily became rich on the results of another's genius.

My father, while still an iron master, during the war of 1812, turned his attention to a subject which has lately obtained the widest and highest prominence, in naval history. He actually invented and patented an Iron Clad monitor war ship. As a matter of interest and curiosity the following extract, giving some historical facts relating to this subject is introduced:

A BALL PROOF VESSEL IN 1814.

Thomas Gregg, of Connelsville, Fayette county, Pennsylvania, invented a *ball proof* vessel in 1813, and received a patent on the 9th March, 1814, which bears the names of James Madison, President; James Monroe, Secretary of State; and Richard Rush, Attorney-General of the United States. This patent was renewed in 1837.

On the Journal of the House of Representatives for Thursday, March 24th, 1814, may be found the following account of proceedings:

"Mr. Wilson presented a memorial of Thomas Gregg, of Pennsylvania, stating, that, he has invented a new *ball proof vessel*, or *floating battery*, and presenting a model for the Examination of Congress, and requesting that its efficiency may be tested by experiment. Ordered, that the said memorial be referred to the Committee on Naval affairs."

A Ball Proof Vessel in 1814.

On Friday, March 25th, 1814, Mr. Lowndes of South Carolina, moved that the Committee on Naval affairs be discharged from the consideration of the petition of Thomas Gregg, and that it be referred to the Secretary of the Navy. This "Mr. Lowndes" conceived a prejudice against the invention, and became, without reason an enemy to Mr. Gregg, using all his influence to defeat his plans.

The model presented, was burned in 1836.

Commodore Dupont, of Delaware, did on one occasion put this vessel to a severe test; and was much pleased with the principle.

He wrote to the Hon. Messrs. A. Stewart and D. Surgen, of Pennsylvania, and Hon. Messrs. John M. Clayton and R. Bayard of Delaware, commending to their favorable notice this valuable invention, and they all concurred in his opinion.

A short extract from the full description and explanations laid before the Authorities, and approved by scientific men, will give the reader some notion of the vessel: "The object is, to make the vessel *ball proof*, and *impenetrable*. In construction, it is framed on an angle of about eighteen degrees, all round the hull. The top timbers elevate the balls, and the lower ones are designed to direct them under the keel. The power is applied between the keels, where there is a concave formed to receive the motive machinery. The power may be reversed to propel the vessel either way. The elevation of her timbers, will be proportioned by her keel and tonnage.

This principle protects men and machinery effectually, and is capable of performing more service than any four vessels now in use, and at one-fourth the usual expense of even one ordinary ship of war, as only eight or ten guns are needed, and men in proportion."

This principle would have saved the government in 1814, $500,000, had it been fairly tested, as the "Fulton" boat proved a perfect failure, which cost that amount: besides, what an immense saving there would have been in human life, as well as treasure.

Congress should look into this matter. Mr. Gregg spent a large amount of money in his efforts to benefit the government, and like many of the truly original men of the country, amassed nothing, and died comparatively poor. A liberal appropriation should be made to his widow, who is in circumstances to appreciate such generosity—or, as it would be in truth an act of sheer justice.

Had Thomas Gregg lived until these days, he, and not the parties who borrowed his idea, would have been recognized as the inventor of "*Iron Clads.*"

My father always said that his invention would only be useful for harbor defence. This idea, time and experience seems to have confirmed, during the past three years, and the judgment of the *original inventor*, is the conclusion of most scientific men to-day.

While sharp competition has been carried on both in France, England and this country, as to who is entitled to the credit of this invention which promises to revolutionize the old established system of naval warfare, I humbly submit, that a reference to the records of the Patent Office at Washington, and to some witnesses who are still living, will incontestably establish the claim of Thomas Gregg, and do justice to his genius, as the real inventor.

At one time my father was comparatively wealthy, but the hand of Providence swept away the fortune he toiled to build up. To this he submitted with becoming philosophy and fortitude, and he afterwards attributed, to this event such a change in his views, as led him to give attention to the concerns of his soul, and to seek the salvation of God.

He was converted on the 23d of March, 1845, upon the summit of a high mountain, near his residence. The spot was notable as being near a large rock. This he afterwards called the "rock of faith." *The following verses written by him convey some account of his experience:*

Burdened with sin, with guilt distressed,
I searched in vain for full release;
But still the weight was on my breast,
I found no joy, or lasting peace.

I wandered to one quiet spot,
And mused with sadness day by day,
The mercy of my God I sought,
And lingered there to weep and pray.

One evening, and the sun went down,
The moon and stars came out above,
And wrestling there with doubt and gloom,
I longed to know a Saviour's love.

A trembling seized upon my frame,
In agony I prayed that night,
When to my troubled spirit came—
The answer, as a flash of light!

With heavenly joy my heart o'erflow'd,
My tongue unloosed, began to praise
The goodness of a pardoning God—
To him this monument I raise.

Now journeying on in blessed hope,
With all my powers to Jesus given,
I trust his grace to raise me up
Redeemed, and saved, at last to heaven.

He became a member of the Protestant Episcopal Church after his conversion, and spent the remnant of an eventful life in the service of God. He died on the 3d day of January, 1854, in the seventy-fifth year of his age, and as I trust, and believe, ripe and ready for an entrance into the mansions of rest.

My mother was born in Western Pennsylvania, and became, at an early age, a member of the Episcopal Church, to which her parents were attached. She still lingers on the shores of time at the age of seventy-six, waiting in Christian hope until her change come. She has been emphatically "a praying mother," presenting her children at the throne of grace, and devoted to their happiness and welfare. I might add much, in relation to her faith in Divine Providence, and her bright experience, after life is ended, that she will rest with Jesus. She has since gone to glory; and I take the liberty of adding an account of her death: Died in Connellsville, Pa., January 14th, 1867, Mrs. Margaret Gregg, in the seventy-eighth year of her age. Converted to God in early life, Mrs. Gregg maintained in its beauty, for more than fifty years, the loveliness of a faithful and consistent Christian character. She lived to see the consecration of two of her sons to the ministry—Revs. Joseph and John C. Gregg, members of the Philadelphia Conference. She was truly a mother in Israel, and at the time of departure her soul seemed to leap across the chasm which separates us from eternity and catch the inspiration so vividly that her farewell words were "Glory! glory!"

CHAPTER II.

CONVERSION.

VISIT TO RELATIONS NEAR WILMINGTON, DEL.—CONVICTION OF SIN—A MOTHER'S PRAYERS—ABOUT TO FLEE LIKE JONAH—ATTENDED PROTRACTED MEETING—SERMON BY DR. CASTLE—BECAME A PUBLIC SEEKER OF RELIGION—REV. S. W. THOMAS—CONVERSION—PROMPTINGS TO DO GOOD—RETURN TO PENNSYLVANIA—THE FAMILY ALTAR—NEIGHBORS CONVERTED—THOUGHTS ABOUT THE MINISTRY—EDUCATION PROFFERED BY THE EPISCOPALIANS.

IN the spring of 1848, I left my Pennsylvania home to visit my uncles, who resided on their farms near Wilmington, Del., and it was while I was in that neighborhood that I became a subject of the saving grace of God. Among the numerous instrumentalities that were employed in leading me to see the error of my ways, and the necessity of a change of heart I attribute to the unceasing prayers of my mother the most important part. While she was engaged pleading for me at a throne of grace, the Spirit powerfully followed me, and convinced me of sin. For three months I sought religion in a secret way, and sincerely desired to become a true Christian. I had been raised to believe in a very quiet kind of religion. I was opposed to noise and excitement, and wanted the blessing in my own way; but like thousands who presume to arrange for themselves the mode of the Holy Spirit's operation, I found no peace.

I determined at this juncture, to go to sea, and informed a pious aunt and my brother, of what I had made up my mind to do. They understood my case, and although I had not revealed to them the state of my feelings, and the burden that lay heavy on my heart, yet they suspected the cause of my restlessness, and at once united in efforts to dissuade me from the course I was about to take. They invited and urged me to accompany them to a protracted meeting then in progress at Mt. Salem M. E. Church near the City of Wilmington. Here my prejudice against night meetings afforded me a pretext to refuse, but my kind aunt persisted in her arguments until I had to consent, out of respect for her, to accompany them to the meeting. I took my seat back near the door, and listened to the sermon. During the prayer-meeting, no less than five different ministers approached me, and urged me to seek salvation. My friends had doubtless sent them to me, but I would not yield that night. I promised the last one that talked with me, however, that if he would let me alone, I would think about the matter, and probably go forward the following night: accordingly, the next night I attended with my aunt, and heard a sermon preached by the Rev. Joseph Castle, D. D., which made a deep impression on my mind. At its close the Rev. Samuel W. Thomas invited me to the altar, saying he would go with me. I then abandoned all my preconceived notions and prejudices, and rose up, and was soon bowed at the altar of prayer, crying to God for mercy. I think I should have been blessed in a few moments, but Satan whispered "not now." The following night I was again at the altar, a great work was in progress, the meeting continued until a late hour, and between 11 and 12 o'clock, God for Christ's sake, converted my soul, and gave me such a clear evidence, that I have never doubted from that hour to the present, the divine change wrought in my heart.

The very first emotions of my mind were to urge and invite others to come to Christ. I joined the Mt. Salem Church the following Sabbath, October 1st, 1849, and felt it to be my duty and privilege to engage in distributing religious books and tracts, in which work I continued for several months. I then returned to Western Pennsylvania to visit my former home, and enjoyed happy seasons with my dear aged mother, in family prayer and religious communion. My heart was stirred to recommend a crucified Saviour to my neighbors and friends, among whom I had been brought up, and the Lord owned my humble instrumentality in a very signal manner. I conducted a protracted meeting where displays of divine power in awakening and conversion, were often witnessed, and a number of my associates were made to rejoice in God.

A conviction rested on my mind that I ought to give myself wholly to the work of calling sinners to repentance. This I resisted, having no desire to become a minister of the gospel; yet I prayed to be directed in the right way. It had often been intimated to me, even before I was converted, that my future course would be that of a preacher. While I was halting at this point, and refusing to go forward in the road Providence seemed to indicate, the members of the church, who had known me all my life, took up my case, and recommended me for license to exhort.

I can look back on a strict moral life from my youth up, and can testify, that from my childhood, the Spirit of God strove with me. I had been in the habit of praying night and morning, during my entire life, before I became experimentally a Christian. Often the impression crossed my mind that God had something for me to do in the world, yet the distinct idea of becoming a Christian minister, was something I could not realize. It seemed so sacred, and so exalted, as to be far beyond my attainment. I have been led, since that time, to believe, that a call to preach the gospel comes not only to the individual ear and conscience, but that there is a concurrent feeling and conviction in the church and community in every case, which will clearly foreshadow the true line of duty to one who is timid in regard to this important matter.

About this time a proposition was made by the Episcopal Church, to give me an education for the ministry of that denomination, but circumstances shaped my course in another direction, whether to my loss or gain, eternity must disclose.

CHAPTER III.

PREACHING.

SECOND VISIT TO DELAWARE—SCHOOL TEACHING—SMYRNA CIRCUIT—LICENSE TO PREACH—SENT TO GREENSBOROUGH CIRCUIT—DR. QUIGLEY—REV. J. B. AYERS—HAPPY TIMES—NUMBERS CONVERTED—ACCOMAC, VIRGINIA—REV. D. DAILEY—REV. CHARLES HILL—DIFFICULTIES WITH SLAVEHOLDERS—REV. A. WALLACE—A SUCCESSFUL YEAR.

IN the summer of 1852, I again visited my uncle's, in Delaware, and engaged in teaching a school in Kent County, within the bounds of the Smyrna Circuit.

Here I was invited to assist the preachers in their Sabbath work, and began to attempt in an humble way preaching the glorious gospel of salvation. One Sabbath evening, at the commencement of a protracted meeting at a place named Kenton, I tried to preach, and the Holy Ghost was present; seventeen persons came forward as seekers of religion, and five of them were that night happily converted.

Thus in Delaware, as well as Pennsylvania, God blessed my labors, before I was licensed to preach, and it is my firm conviction, that every member of the church ought to work for Christ, in seeking to save souls, and they would be rewarded with much fruit; if active in the cause.

At the last Quarterly Conference of this year for Smyrna Circuit, I was examined, and received license as a Local preacher in the M. E. Church. Rev. T. J. Quigley, D. D. was the Presiding Elder, and Rev. Brothers T. Newman and Joseph Gregg the traveling preachers on the circuit.

In the spring of 1853, I was sent as junior preacher, with Rev. J. B. Ayers in charge, to Greensborough Circuit. We had a pleasant and profitable year's work, having had over one hundred souls converted and added to the church. I received much kindness from Dr. Quigley and Bro. Ayers during this year; both are true friends and wise counsellors of young men.

In the spring of 1854, I was employed by Rev. D. Dailey, Presiding Elder of the Snow Hill District, and appointed to Accomac Circuit, Eastern Shore of Virginia. The Rev. C. Hill was preacher in charge, and a finer colleague no young man need ever desire. God blessed our labors during the year with some revivals, although vice and sin abounded, and some of the people, who profess godliness, were so wedded to the idol of slavery, and so sensitive when strangers were among them, that they were more ready to watch for, and abuse abolitionists than to say their prayers. Some of this class professed not to like me, because they suspected my principles, which were to befriend their poor oppressed and neglected slaves; and I can assure them there was no love lost. They respected me fully as much as I could find it in my heart to esteem any man or woman, who claimed absolute ownership in human beings, made and redeemed by the same God and Saviour with themselves, and who without the least compunction, bought, sold, traded, whipped, and ruthlessly separated families of these suffering people, as if they had no feelings of attachment to localities, or relations, among themselves.

The accursed spirit of slavery, which subsequently culminated in the great rebellion, was a fruitful source of strife at that time in Accomac. Misrepresentations and slanders were originated there about me, which for some years were retailed about, and repeated to my disparagement by some of my own brethren, before the Philadelphia Conference.

Time has wrought wondrous changes in old Virginia. Where are now the "bullies" and "rowdies," who used to go about to our meetings, cursing the Methodist preachers, and calling them opprobrious names? Gone in the whirlwind of the rebellion! Dead! most of them, having fallen under a traitor's flag, and their blasphemies with them down to a rebel's grave! And the man they would have lynched, still lives, and lives to rejoice over the downfall of rebeldom, and the extirpation from this fair land of slavery.

To the glory of God, I record the conversion of over one hundred immortal souls, that eventful year. With my beloved colleague I labored in harmony, and spent many pleasant hours with Rev. Adam Wallace, on the adjacent charge. He has been, since the first day I knew him my steadfast friend, and I hope our acquaintance begun on earth, may be continued throughout an endless eternity. To him I accord the praise justly due, for his candor, in showing me the faults and deficiencies of character which, in common with most young men, retarded my progress and usefulness. His words to me have often been the counsels of a true friend and brother. I have enjoyed the benefit of correspondence with him through all the subsequent years and changing events of my career thus far. I collected one hundred dollars during the year for my venerable Presiding Elder, Brother Dailey, to assist him in buying a home for himself and wife. Soon after this year he retired from the active work, and has since died and gone to glory.

CHAPTER IV.

THE ITINERANCY.

RECEIVED ON TRIAL IN THE PHILADELPHIA ANNUAL CONFERENCE—APPOINTED TO BERLIN CIRCUIT, MD.—REV. WM. MERRILL—RESULTS OF PROTRACTED MEETINGS—LARGE INCREASE—CONFERENCE OF 1856—APPOINTED TO CHURCH CREEK CIRCUIT WITH REV. H. SANDERSON—NEW SABBATH SCHOOLS ORGANIZED—CIRCULATION OF PERIODICALS—ELECTION DAY—A YOUNG LAWYER SNUBBED—CAMP MEETING SCENES—A DISTURBER SETTLED.

IN the spring of 1855, I was received on trial by the Philadelphia Annual Conference of the Methodist Episcopal Church, a body of ministers, who for intelligence, patriotism, and zeal, are not surpassed in the known world. The honor of having my name on the record of such a body I estimate as the highest which man can aspire to on earth. With this privilege, however, there are responsibilities which may well lead a young man to inquire "who is sufficient for these things?"

My appointment was announced with the Rev. Wm. Merrill, for Berlin Circuit in Worcester County, Maryland. This was a large and laborious field of labor. Extra meetings began in September, and were continued until the following March. All the churches were visited in turn, and the result of revival efforts was about two hundred and seventy-five souls who professed to be converted to God, two hundred of whom united with the church on probation.

I was greatly encouraged this year by such wonderful scenes of the outpouring of the Spirit as were witnessed all around us. My colleague labored hard and with great success.

At the conference commencing March 26th, 1856, I enjoyed happy seasons, intermingling with my brethren, and at its close received my next appointment to Church Creek Circuit, with the Rev. Henry Sanderson, as preacher in charge,

This circuit was about thirty miles in extent, and embraced some ten or twelve appointments. Several of these were on little islands, to reach which, we had to traverse marshes, and use the indispensable canoe. In the summer season, the people were greatly pestered with mosquitoes, and myriads of other flies, which swarmed in every place, irritating both man and beast, sometimes to a degree of frenzy. In the winter, this region of the country was very desolate, and the roads were in shocking condition with mud. Yet we had a successful year's work, and took into church fellowship over one hundred.

Three new Sabbath Schools were organized, and a fine large list of subscribers obtained for our excellent Church paper, the Christian Advocate and Journal. The people we found to be warm-hearted, hospitable, and very kind. The spirit of secession which I learn, has since that time, turned many away from the old paths, had not then begun its diabolical work.

On election day I went to the polls, to do what every good citizen has the right to do—that is, vote. A young limb of the law, assumed to be dictator as to whether, and *where* I ought to vote. His interference on that occasion, reacted slightly on his own head. I felt my manhood, doubled my fist, and after giving him the benefit of a short special sermon, coolly walked up and deposited my ballot in the name of constitutional liberty. Had the gentleman supposed I was going to vote for his favorite, James Buchanan, there would have been no objection. And this is the reason some shallow-pated partizans raise the hue and cry against Methodist preachers being politicians, because they dare act for themselves, and be independent, and far seeing enough not to be led by the nose in this matter.

We held a Camp Meeting this year, and among other incidents which I recall, was one of a poor ignorant, vicious fellow, who persisted in coming in around the altar, interrupting the exercises, until, as a religious necessity I had to drag him forth, and pitch him over a fence.

It was my rule at all our protracted meetings, to keep the peace, when disorderly characters were around, and threatening to be troublesome. God has given me a stout frame, and a strong arm, and the rowdies generally gave me a wide berth, when we were likely to come to close quarters.

CHAPTER V.

CHURCH BUILDING.

ORDAINED DEACON—A "BREAK NECK HILL" APPOINTMENT—CHARACTER OF BLACKWATER CIRCUIT—WHISKY DRINKING PEOPLE—THE BLUES—MY FIRST SABBATH—GLOOMY PROSPECT—GOOD RESOLUTIONS—ACTIVE WORK—THREE CHURCHES TO BE REBUILT—ONE NEW CHURCH TO BE ERECTED—THE WORK BEGINS, PROCEEDS—AND IS COMPLETED—DEDICATION OF AIREY'S CHAPEL—FREEBORN GARRETSON—OLD TIMES—DOCTORS ROBERTS AND WILLIAMS—SUCCESS—DEDICATION OF SCOTT'S CHAPEL—GRIFFITHS—REVIVAL—A HARVEST TIME—THE NEW CHURCH—REV. A MANSHIP—"GREGG CHAPEL"—A GOOD DEDICATION—CAMP MEETING—ARRAY OF PREACHERS—GREAT POWER—SUMMING UP OF A SUCCESSFUL YEAR—SECOND YEAR ON BLACKWATER CIRCUIT—ANOTHER CAMP MEETING—MINISTERS PRESENT—OPPOSITION, AND THE WEAPONS USED TO CONQUER IT—REV. DR. THOMPSON—CLOSE OF MY TERM.

At the Conference in the spring of 1857—after due examination, and a solemn charge from the presiding Bishop, I was received into full connection, and elected, and ordained a Deacon in the Church of God, by the venerable Bishop Waugh. My destination this year was a little circuit called "Blackwater," embracing part of Dorchester County, Md., and lying between Cambridge and Vienna. I had been looking over the pages of a book entitled "My Father Braddock," and thought the title and description of "Break neck hill" appointment, suited my new field of labor exactly. There were, all told but seventeen members, that I could identify in the whole charge, and most of them were poor in circumstances, and unable to do much toward my support.

The few churches were in a miserably dilapidated condition, and through long neglect, for they were cut off from adjacent circuits, and set adrift, it was difficult to draw the people together to hear preaching. Indeed I was informed on my way to this locality, that the favorite Sunday pastime of the people was hunting musk rats, and drinking whisky, a representation which I found by actual observation to be not far from the truth.

This was then properly a mission field, but there was no appropriation made towards its cultivation, and I had to take the situation of things as I found them, go to work with all my might, or turn away discouraged, and cease to be a traveling preacher. At first I was disheartened. I had thoughts which were not at all complimentary to those by whose authority I had been appointed. The Presiding Elders and the Bishop, I suppose, sent me, and it was a strong conviction in my mind for a time, that somebody had made a mistake. Filled with gloom I repaired to my work, and shall never forget my first Sabbath's labors. It was a rainy, dull, morning; about twenty persons were out to hear the new preacher. The rain poured down, the house leaked badly, the doors were off the hinges, and things in general were in an unhinged state.

Cheerfulness predominates in my disposition, and it was well for me that day that I was enabled to look on the brightest side of the case, and avoid a severe attack of the blues. A kind-hearted gentleman invited me home with him to dinner, and the continued rain prevented my filling the afternoon appointment.

While musing in that gentleman's parlor that gloomy Sunday, I thought of the happiness of my previous years, and contrasted them with my present prospects, until my reflections began to take a sour turn, and I was tempted to think, with the enemies of our Methodist economy, that injustice and oppression are often the only reward of faithful labor, and a wide departure from the strict impartiality we should expect in the appointing power, is bearing hard on some, while others are favored, flattered, and always receive choice appointments. I confess to be somewhat ashamed now to recall the course of my reflections. I ought to have remembered that *some one* must go to the poor places,—that no place was so wretched that it might not be made better, and that what seems darkest to us, is God's way to prove our faith, and bless our souls. The result of two years on this little cast-off charge, now convinces me, as it will the most sceptical, that Divine Providence rules our appointments, and in no place within our bounds, could I have found a field of toil more ripe for the harvest, or better adapted to my temperament, and personal religious improvement, than "Blackwater Circuit."

I saw that something must be done to make the

churches attractive and comfortable; to rouse up the people to exertion and hope; and inspire them with fortitude, as well as myself, in meeting the apparently insurmountable difficulties, by which we seemed to be surrounded. So, after prayer to God for assistance and direction, I remembered the days of Nehemiah, and resolved that I would try to build up the walls and waste places of Zion, trusting in his God for help.

I soon found favor in the eyes of the people, and engaged workmen to superintend the rebuilding of three of our old churches, named Airey's, Scott's and Griffith's, and also procured a builder from Baltimore to erect a new church at a point where it was agreed that we needed and must have a place of worship. I soon found my hands full, with four churches under way, and the workmen all looking to me for the money necessary to meet expenses, as they accrued every week. I was enabled by driving early and late, to meet my engagements, and satisfy all parties. The work had to be done with the best materials, and in the best manner, and in due time we rejoiced together over our complete success.

Airey's Chapel was originally named after the family of that name, who were the early and steadfast friends of Freeborn Garretson, and it was in this vicinity that he was arrested for preaching the Gospel, by the Sheriff of Dorchester County, and carried to Cambridge jail, from which he preached and exhorted the people through the iron bars of his prison-window, until they were compelled to release him, and let him proceed on his mission, as the pioneer of Methodism through this region of country.

I felt it to be no insignificant honor that the work of rebuilding this old time-honored and historical church devolved on me. The amount expended on it was five hundred and fifty dollars.

We secured the services of the Rev. Dr. Roberts, of Baltimore, and the Rev. Dr. Williams, of Cornersville, Maryland, for the dedication; both preached with power; we had a glorious time, and every cent of the indebtedness was cheerfully raised at the morning service.

Scott's Chapel about the same time was completed, at a cost of about five hundred and forty dollars, and was rededicated by the Rev. J. Dickerson of the Philadelphia Conference; Rev. John Hersey, and the Rev. Dr. Thompson of Cambridge, also giving their aid; we all felt happy; for Christ was in our midst, and this church, like Airey's, was presented to God free of debt. In connection with this building there was a tract of land which had been donated to the church, but which a certain person claimed to belong to him. We had to "Sheriff" him to obtain our rights, and succeeded in regaining the property, clearing up our title, and making this covetous party pay the costs of the suit.

Our new Church in the neighborhood of the Nanticoke River was duly finished, and the day of dedication appointed. This service was performed by the excellent and original Rev. Andrew Manship of the Philadelphia Conference.

Although the weather turned out to be unfavorable, yet the people were there in troops, and the preacher interested all, in his usual happy style, until many shouted "glory to God." All the money we needed was raised in the morning, and besides, twenty-five persons gave each one dollar to Bro. M. to make me a life director of the Tract Society, which he represented.

The Trustees then, after consultation, insisted on a name for the new church. They communicated their desire to Brother Manship, and he baptized the place as GREGG CHAPEL, a name which it has borne ever since. This was against my consent, but they would have it so, and so it is.

Griffith's Church now remained to be completed, and this was soon done, at an outlay of one hundred and fifty dollars. The ministers engaged to officiate, having failed to reach the church on account of inclement weather, the task of rededication devolved on myself. The money was all collected at the meeting in the morning. In the evening I preached again and invited souls to Christ; and there were over thirty persons converted in less than one week. This occurred during the busy season of wheat harvest, and was to us a glorious ingathering of souls; to God be all the praise.

Thus by the Divine blessing, on which I cast my reliance at the outset, we succeeded in having three churches rebuilt at an outlay of over twelve hundred dollars, and in erecting a neat new church, which cost over one thousand dollars; all the work was accomplished, the funds raised, and bills paid, in less than five months from the time I arrived upon the circuit. The result gladdened my own, and the hearts of the people, and we never lacked for good congregations, good collections, and happy meetings, while I remained among them.

In this connection I might add, that I assisted the colored people to the extent of my ability in building one new church, and rebuilding another, both of which I had the pleasure to dedicate for them. This, of course, offended some of the rabid pro-slavery party, who were extremely sensitive and jealous, about extending any notice, help, or encouragement to these poor people. What I did, thank God, I was not afraid or ashamed to do, as a minister of the Lord Jesus Christ, who owns, among this class of persons, many jewels of Christian piety, who, when their proud oppressors shall be forgotten, will stand before the throne, clothed in white robes, having come up through great tribulation.

We held a Camp Meeting on the Circuit, consisting of one hundred and twenty tents, white and colored. The following preachers rallied round me, and preached with great power and success: Rev. H. Colclazer, Presiding Elder, Rev. J. Dickerson, Rev. H. Sanderson, and Rev. J. B. Quigg, of my own Conference; Rev. J. W. Cullum, Rev. Mr. Thrush, and Rev. Prof. Hank, of the Baltimore Conference. We had excellent order.

There was such manifestations of the presence and influence of the Spirit, that promenading was abandoned, and even despisers were led to wonder and tremble before the power of God. A great many found peace in believing, and the tented grove was to us all a place of great rejoicing.

In summing up the results of that year, which began so gloomy, I find that the people raised and paid about two thousand, five hundred, and fifty-six dollars, for church building, missionary and tract cause, and other demands made upon them, besides several hundred dollars, collected among the people of color, to pay off their church liabilities.

I have always endeavored to extend the circulation of our religious literature wherever I have been, and even on this comparatively barren field, I obtained a large number of subscribers for the "Advocate." Out of the number converted to God this year, one hundred united with us in church fellowship, and the year closed up in great peace and, as the reader cannot fail to perceive, in unexpected and most signal prosperity. Surely "God moves in a mysterious way, His wonders to perform."

In the Spring of 1858, I was reappointed to Blackwater Circuit, and this time went to my charge with very different emotions from what I experienced the preceding year. The work moved on, the congregations were large, and the classes were well attended.

We held another Camp Meeting, having one hundred and twenty-five tents. The ministers in attendance were

Rev. William L. Gray, Rev. H. Colclazer, Rev. A. Manship and Rev. T. J. Thompson, all of whom preached with life and liberty, and success crowned their efforts in extending the Redeemer's kingdom.

During my two years' work on this Circuit, the chief opposition I met with was from ministers of other denominations, *slave-holders*, and the *Devil*. I had occasionally to fall back on the inalienable rights of man, and defend myself, by collaring the uncivilized, and shaking them into decent behaviour—when moral suasion failed of effect.

I found a friend and valuable helper in the Rev. Dr. Thompson, of Cambridge—father of Rev. C. I. Thompson of the Philadelphia Conference, who manifested an abiding interest in the spiritual welfare of the people. And they with myself will long remember him for his kindness and attention. My second year closed, with what was regarded as "a good report."

CHAPTER VI.

ORDINATION.

ANNUAL CONFERENCE—ORDAINED ELDER—WICONISCO—MOUNTAINS—CHURCH DEBT PAID—FESTIVAL—INGATHERING TO THE CHURCH—WARM FRIENDS—HUMMELSTOWN—CHURCH REPAIRED—RE-OPENING—REV. MESSRS. BISHOP, HEILNER, AND CARSON—MISSIONARY COLLECTION—ASTOUNDING STINGINESS—A FREE GOSPEL—REFLECTIONS—OPPOSITION TO REVIVALS—A "PETER CARTWRIGHT" ARGUMENT—VICTORY ON THE LORD'S SIDE.

THE Annual Conference of 1859 convened in Philadelphia, on the 26th day of March, and was to me a very pleasant and memorable session. The "course of study" prescribed for young preachers, and the annual examination in committee-room was now completed. After due representation in my case I was elected to Elders' orders, and on Sabbath, the 29th of March, 1859, I was ordained by the Rev. Bishop Scott, in company with the class of 1855, with each of whom I was happy to be associated, and will always rejoice to name them among my special friends.

My appointment this year was to Wiconisco among the mountains of Dauphin County, Pa., where, as Rev. John F. Chaplain informed my friends in Cambridge, Md., the sun does not rise until ten o'clock in the morning! Indeed a greater contrast in scenery could hardly be imagined than that between my fields of labor for the past few years, and that to which I was now assigned. Instead of low lands, level marshes, and the ebb and flow of tides, I was surrounded with lofty hills, rapid rivers, delightful and healthy atmosphere, and stirring enterprise.

Our church at this place being in debt and the money to pay it needed, my first duty was to confer with the Trustees in regard to raising the necessary funds. We determined to make an effort, and accordingly, after my first sermon, the congregation were asked to contribute one hundred dollars. This amount was given in a few minutes, and we were much encouraged to go forward.

On the Fourth of July we had a public celebration. The ladies were exceedingly active in preparations for a good time, and with the most commendable zeal, they provided a sumptuous dinner, from the proceeds of which enough money was obtained to pay off the entire debt remaining on the church.

The year passed away pleasantly. The people were extremely kind to me, and their names are still cherished in memory among my best Christian friends. We did not forget the interests of our church periodicals, raised a large missionary collection, and received into the church sixty-nine probationers as the result of a gracious revival.

In the spring of 1860, I was appointed to Hummelstown Circuit, and found the work to be very laborious. The appointments were several miles apart, and I had often to ride twenty-five miles and preach three times the same day.

We repaired the Hummelstown church and had a good bell placed upon it, then arranged for special service at the re-opening. It was an occasion of great interest. The Rev. Wm. Bishop, of Harrisburg, Rev. S. A. Heilner, of Lykens, Pa., and Rev. Robert J. Carson, of the Philadelphia Conference, officiated with acceptability and profit. All the money asked for was cheerfully contributed, and this enterprise throughout was a success.

At one of my appointments on the circuit I made special arrangements for a grand missionary collection, and secured the services of a certain Rev. M. D., to preach the sermon. He performed his part with ability, and to his astonishment, when the offerings of the people were received, and all the funds carefully counted, the result of the appeal and all our previous plans, was, the sum of one hundred and fifty cents, to send the word of life to the perishing heathen!!

There was in a certain locality a wealthy gentleman of Dutch descent, who professed to be a great friend and admirer of the preacher. He regularly attended my ministry with his family, and I was regarded as quite a favorite. At the close of the year, my good friend was solicited by one of the stewards for a liberal contribution towards the support of the gospel. I suppose he made it a subject of careful thought, if not of prayer, before he came forward with his amount: but when it did appear, it consisted of the handsome (?) sum of twenty-five cents, for one year's preaching to him and his house the unsearchable riches of Christ!

He is one of the many—I am glad to think the number is growing less every year, who believe in a *free* gospel, and are afraid to connect themselves with any denomination of Christians, from the dread of current expenses, and their innate stinginess of soul, regarding every call and claim of benevolence in the light of a nuisance, and living, laboring, and saving only for self. With such, the love of money becomes an absorbing mania; and a man of this stripe will even deny himself and his family the common necessaries of life, through this vice of avarice, and a growing fear of coming want. They do not reflect on the meanness involved in *stealing* their preaching, by dodging around, without a regular Church home, and in evading the Scriptural obligation to support the ministers of God.

Another class of people, however, go even beyond this. They oppose, by every means, the progress of a living, real Christianity; and such a thing as revival operations, is to them a source of torment. They are the fitting, and willing tools of the Devil, who employs and assists them. I had several encounters with both ministers and members of other denominations this year, and by God's help, we not only withstood their rage, but pushed the conquest of the cross into their own lines, and had a number of our enemies converted in our revival meetings, who united with us, and learned to shout the praise of that God, who had opened their blinded eyes, and brought them, by his Spirit, into a blessed and happy experience.

During the progress of our meeting at Manada Furnace, some of the blue—or rather *green*—mountain boys were influenced, as I was led to believe, by members of other churches, to attend our services, with the design of interrupting the meeting. I had read some sketches of the Rev. Peter Cartwright, D. D., and at once concluded to adopt his tactics in the premises.

A strong guard was stationed in and around the church. The preacher had to seize hold of an unruly fellow occasionally; and thus by placing ourselves on the defensive, and prosecuting some of the ringleaders, their old-fogy abettors, and bigoted parents, who belong to a certain church, but are totally ignorant of true religion, were foiled and disappointed.

The work of God moved on, and both here and at Hummelstown, we had a glorious meeting, and gathered quite a large number into the fellowship of the Methodist faith, whom, may the God of our Fathers bless, and establish, until, after a life of zeal for his cause on earth, they gain

—"The blest fields, on the banks of the river,
And shout hallelujah, for ever, and ever."

CHAPTER VII.

LOYALTY.

APPOINTED TO BAINBRIDGE—REVIVAL—REAPPOINTED—COMMISSIONED CHAPLAIN—PRESENTED WITH A BEAUTIFUL SWORD—OFF TO THE FIELD—RETURN—APPOINTED TO MONTGOMERY SQUARE—OPPOSITION—AN OLD DISLOYAL FARMER—BISHOP HOPKINS ON SLAVERY—REVIVAL—AN INCIDENT—VISIT TO PRESIDENT LINCOLN—INTERVIEW WITH SECESSIONISTS—A JEW NONPLUSSED—RUNNING THE CHURCHES—ESTIMATE OF MR. LINCOLN—NOMINATED FOR HOSPITAL CHAPLAIN—CONFIRMED—ORDERED TO DEPARTMENT OF THE GULF—A WORD TO "ALL WHOM IT MAY CONCERN."

AT the Conference held March 20th, 1861, I received my appointment to Bainbridge, Pa. This is a pleasant village located on the east bank of the Susquehanna river. As usual in all our smaller towns in this region, denominational lines were strictly drawn here. My first and constant desire in all my appointments, was to labor in harmony with my fellow-Christians, and live on terms of peace with all who love our Lord Jesus Christ, but to press forward in the work of getting sinners converted. Where offense has been taken at the mode I employ, and professed ministers of the gospel, arise to oppose the work through prejudice, or a fear that their own fabric may be invaded, and fall down before the onset of Holy Ghost religion, I simply move on, in the course I deem best, and think it useless to open controversies, or engage in arguments, while souls are perishing. Through much opposition, I had the pleasure of seeing a good work at Bainbridge, and many souls were added to the Lord.

I was returned to the same charge in 1862. At this period the Nation had become aroused to the magnitude of the rebellion, and all the true friends of Liberty and Union had to speak out, and *act out* their convictions.

Of my own record, since the firing of the first gun that inaugurated the slave-holders' rebellion, I have no reason to be ashamed. On the 16th of August, in this year, I was appointed and commissioned Chaplain of the one hundred and twenty-seventh Regiment Pennsylvania Volunteers, by his excellency, Governor Andrew Gregg Curtin.

My regiment was under marching orders, and I had to bid my congregation farewell. After preaching to them on the Sunday evening before my departure, I was presented with a magnificent sword, by the following worthy and patriotic gentlemen, as a token of their esteem: Dr. R. H. Jones of Bainbridge, Prof. Samuel Eby of Elizabethtown, Pa., and Abraham Collins, Esq., merchant of Falmouth. This offended some of the friends of Jeff. Davis, in that community, but their wrath was of no account, in view of the overwhelming tide of loyal sentiment in good old Lancaster County. May God bless all her patriotic sons and daughters.

Of my adventures and experiences in the army, the reader of these pages will find a full account in the proper place. My term of service expired in the spring of 1863, when, returning to my Conference and regular work, I was sent to Montgomery Square, a pleasant station, in the vicinity of Philadelphia. I found here some of the kindest Christian people I have known, and spent a very happy term among them.

As I had been in the army, of course I was a mark for the hatred of rebel sympathizers. One man, lately from the city, where he had experienced some rough usage on account of his Southern proclivities, tried to strengthen his cause by misrepresentation and slander of me; but my people were not disposed to ignore a true Union man, or be influenced against one who had served his country in the field, by a weak, although wealthy advocate for the "institution" of slavery.

This person had the assurance to distribute copies of Bishop Hopkins' book, wherever he could find a reader, and went so far as to deposit them in the front yards of some of my members. He and all the hissing tribe who followed his counsel, failed to do me the slightest injury. I was enabled to move forward with steady steps, and God blessed us in the work of revival. We had a meeting of extraordinary power. The word of the Lord spread like fire in dry stubble. Over fifty souls were converted, and what is remarkable, there were several among the number who were over sixty years of age.

After preaching on the morning of Christmas day, I was about to dismiss the congregation, when, to my surprise, one of the stewards rose and requested the people to be seated, as he wished their attention for a few moments. He then addressed himself to me, in a neat speech, and in the name of those who were attendants on my ministry, presented me with a pocket book containing fifty dollars in greenbacks; and in the name of the young ladies of the congregation, a beautiful pair of gloves. I tried to return my thanks for such substantial tokens of sympathy and confidence, and remarked that the feelings which prompted such generosity were of more real value than anything else. I was happy to know that I was surrounded by such kind people.

On the 18th day of February, 1864, I visited Washington, and was permitted to have an interview with President Lincoln. I shall never forget a scene I witnessed on that occasion. It endeared that honored man to my heart, and gave me a strong impression of his wisdom and firmness in dealing with the enemies of the Government.

While I was seated in his office, a lady who was a secessionist, and a resident of Washington City, forced herself into his presence, and approaching him said:

"Mr. President, my son is a prisoner of war, and he now desires to take the oath of allegiance."

"Under what circumstances was your son captured?" inquired Mr. Lincoln.

"While on his way to the rebel army, sir," the lady replied.

"Pray, where had he been?"

"In Washington, sir," she answered, "he having returned home sick."

Mr. Lincoln then said, "You kept him concealed in your house—fattened him up—and then sent him back to the rebel army to assist in destroying this government; and further, madam, I have no confidence in you, or your son."

"But, sir," said she, "my son is a reliable man."

"No doubt he was," Mr. Lincoln replied, "when he had a rebel musket on his shoulder."

This ended the dialogue, and the lady retired.

Soon another party entered the apartment—a Jew, accompanied by a lady and gentleman. The Jew approached the president and said:

"Mr. Lincoln, this lady is the wife of a rebel Captain who is now a prisoner, and he desires to take the oath of allegiance."

The President looked the Jew in the face, saying:

"The Captain has become quite penitent, I suppose, since he has been captured by our forces," and added: "he is too big a fish for me to allow to take the oath, and thereby extend to him a chance to return to the rebel army the first opportunity regardless of his oath, as many of them have done already."

The Jew said; "Mr. President, he is perfectly reliable."

"I believe that," responded Mr. Lincoln, "when in command of a company of rebel soldiers."

"But, sir, I will vouch for him," said the Jew.

"And pray, sir," said Mr. Lincoln, "who are you?"

The man answered that he kept a store in Washington, and that he was acquainted with Mrs. Lincoln. The President inquired where he became acquainted with Mrs. Lincoln.

"At my place of business, sir," said he.

Mr. Lincoln remarked that he did not believe that he knew Mrs. L. At the same moment he rang the bell, and a messenger appeared, whom he directed to go and ask Mrs. Lincoln if she was acquainted with Mr.—— The messenger soon returned, and informed him that she said she did not know such a man.

The President looked the embarrassed Jew in the eye, and said, "Do you hear that Mr.——? Now, sir, you can leave."

On the 24th of March, 1864, Mr. Lincoln, in a conversation between himself, Mr. Stanton and a certain Bishop, informed them that he had not engaged to "run the churches."

I recall these incidents, to show the impartiality and sagacity he displayed in his administration during the deepest trials of the country. My opinion is that there was not a man in the civilized world who was as true a representative of republicanism as the Honorable and now revered Abraham Lincoln.

Honest as a politician, pure as a patriot, devout and humble in the sense of his dependence on, and accountability to the great God, he has well deserved the title so generally accorded to him, as "the second Washington."

On the 18th of February, 1864, I was nominated by this great and good President for the position of Hospital Chaplain, and my appointment was sent to the Senate of the United States for confirmation.

Pending action in my case, I attended the session of Conference in Wilmington, Del., and was by Bishop Ames appointed to Guthrieville Circuit. In two days after this was announced, my appointment as a Chaplain was confirmed by the Senate. On the 18th of March, I received my commission from the President, and was ordered by the Surgeon-General to report for duty to the Medical Director of the Department of the Gulf, for assignment to one of the General Hospitals in New Orleans, La. This change of programme I believed to be in accordance with the will and direction of Providence, and immediately turned my attention to the new sphere of duty which had opened before me. Bishop Ames kindly transferred me from the charge to which I had been assigned, and gave his concurrence to my appointment as Chaplain in the United States Army.

The above will explain why I did not go to my field of labor; for I wish it distinctly understood that I have never refused to do the work, or go to the post of duty assigned me by the Bishop and his council. The supposition by some that I did not go to the Guthrieville Circuit because it was regarded as a poor and unpromising field of labor, is far from being correct. All my appointments in the past were understood to be among the hardest portions of our work, but I have labored cheerfully, and by the blessing of God, have tried to bring up, and improve every place I have occupied. I may also say, for the information of all whom it may concern, that I never received more than one hundred and fifty dollars besides my board and traveling expenses, on any charge, and very frequently less than that. It will be seen, therefore, that I have had no very special favors from the appointing power, but I have acted as an obedient son in the gospel, and do not regret that I have labored, suffered, and borne reproach for the sake of our common Master and his blessed cause.

CHAPTER VIII.

PERSONAL.

VIEWS ON THE EFFICIENCY OF THE MINISTRY—COMMON SENSE AND LIVING FAITH BETTER THAN DEAD LANGUAGES—REVIVALS OF RELIGION SANCTIONED BY SCRIPTURE—MISSION OF METHODISM—PERSONAL—KINDNESS OF FRIENDS—REV. JAMES RIDDLE—REMARKABLE PROVIDENCES—RESCUE FROM DROWNING—FALL FROM A HORSE—ESCAPE FROM ROBBERS—THE GLORY GIVEN TO GOD.

BEFORE concluding this department of my book, I have thought it would not be out of place for me to write down some reflections, which have long occupied my mind, respecting an efficient ministry.

Is it absolutely necessary that a man converted and called of God to preach repentance and the remission of sins to his dying fellow-men, must turn aside from the work to which the Holy Spirit and his ardent nature prompts him, and settle down to the study of Greek, Latin, or Hebrew? Must he spend a few valuable years of his fresh and vigorous youth in learning philosophy, figuring abstract problems, or plodding wearily over the pages of old Pagan poets? "Gaining knowledge," said the wise and practical Wesley, "is a good thing, but saving souls is better." I do not undervalue learning, but simply inquire whether that species called the classics is essential to success in the Methodist itinerancy?

The controversy on this subject is waxing warmer every year, and some probabilities seem to point in the direction of a collegiate course, as a prerequisite for admission into an annual conference, and the regular work of the Methodist pastorate. Some of the bishops, it is said, favor this arrangement, and editors, presidents, and the whole corps of college professors clap their hands in glee, and say "amen" to it.

There is, moreover, a kind of distinction springing up between brethren, which, if allowed to obtain, will prove very unbecoming, and will serve to bring us into contempt before the world, as a house divided against itself. The new-fledged graduate, no matter what amount of brains he may possess, is often seen stepping around on the stilts of his supposed superiority, and putting on airs in the presence of his fellow-laborers, who have no "A. M." or "B. A." tagged on to their names, which is calculated to bring them into discredit.

My candid opinion is, that we have as good men, and as great men, in every respect, who never studied the dead languages, as any who boast of proficiency in that direction. Colleges never did, and never will, give a man brains; nor can they impart a deeper endowment of holy earnestness, or the unction of the Spirit, which qualifies for most eminent success. The larger portion of our clergy, still, are of that class whom I denominate self-educated men.

The generations of our predecessors,—men who shook this continent by their power, came forth, not from seminaries, but from shoe-benches, and the plough; from humble and ordinary occupations, hardy through toil, happy in the enjoyment of good health, and, above all, men of one work, for which God called them, and to which they were baptized with the Holy Ghost and fire sent down from heaven.

When the day comes, if it ever does arrive in the history of American Methodism, that shall witness a rule requiring every young man who feels moved to take upon himself the work of preaching the gospel, to turn his attention first to the study of Greek and Hebrew, the cause of Christ and perishing souls will suffer, and the ardor, freshness, and power of such young men will, by entering a college as students, wane and languish, and some of them will either backslide, or become a dry literary incumbrance on the church.

What I mean, is, so far as my observation has extended, self-educated men are fully up to the standard by which we should test ministerial character, and are often successful and generally useful among the masses, and are found to be available for the conversion of this world of sinners to God. They should not be discarded; nor should unkind reflections be cast upon them, and on the Fathers of Methodism, by this modern hue and cry about the need of Colleges, Universities, and Biblical Institutes. If the common sense that characterized the brave old legions of a past generation shall descend on their sons and successors, and like them, we be men of simplicity in manner, energy of action, and self-sacrifice for the promotion of holiness through all the land, we can take the world for Christ. I do not argue against classical education, or despise the gaining of knowledge, but, while I admire, and wish great good to the "D. D's.," and bid the educators God speed, I think the hardest and largest part of our work must be done by men who, instead of "recitations," and speculations, and parchment credentials, shall live and labor for eternity, and spend their short life in the most practical manner of glorifying God, and whose highest ambition is to hear at last the Master say, "Well done, good and faithful servant."

On the subject of revivals of religion, I desire to present a few words. I am a firm advocate of these "times of refreshing," and believe in the outpouring of the Spirit on set and special occasions, in answer to prayer, and the use of the means appointed and improved, for bringing awakened souls to the cross, and uniting God's people in faith, love, and zeal.

The ministry of the Apostles was honored with frequent baptisms of the Holy Ghost, and we learn that under revival efforts and influences, much people were added to the Lord. Through all the history and progress of the true church of Jesus Christ, we have illustrations of the value, and indeed the absolute necessity of awakening and saving grace.

How then can any lover of Christ oppose a work of this kind? We ought to rejoice and be exceeding glad, instead of grumbling and fault finding, when we see the tide of salvation rising, and rolling on in majestic power, sometimes including whole neighborhoods, and falling on both the aged and the young in its soul-saving influence.

My own soul was converted to God at a revival of religion, and I have witnessed the conversion of large numbers of others during my ministry, when the power of the gospel was manifested to save.

As a church, we should never ignore them. Our growth in numbers, and success in every department, has been through the instrumentality of revivals. Millions on earth and in heaven to-day, were awakened, converted, and brought into the fold of Christ on these occasions, and, if summoned to give their testimony, would tell of many a camp meeting, or protracted effort, where they were saved, and without which, in all probability, they would never have been aroused to the need of regeneration by the Spirit. I have in these pages frequently observed, that ministers and members of certain denominations where I have labored, did all they could, to discredit the work, and oppose all who were in favor of spiritual Christianity. What manner of men are they, who stand all the day idle, themselves, half asleep, or wholly indifferent to the salvation of the people, and when they are waked up, by the noise of sinners crying for mercy, or saints of God shouting on the battles of Immanuel, get angry, and growl over it, calling it wild-fire, enthusiasm, and fanatical folly, and warning their own poor bigoted, sober-sided, and deluded followers, to have nothing to do with these Methodists? That we are and ought to be enthusiasts I admit, but that there is either fanaticism or folly in our modes of operation I take the liberty to deny. We are a missionary church, and intend, in obedience to the command of the Captain of our salvation, to battle on against every opposition that may be employed by earth or hell; and as sure as truth is on our side, error shall fade and fall before us; spirituality shall increase, and warm into life, the cold, dead formality by which many churches and some parts of our own is paralyzed. We cannot, we dare not, allow souls for whom Christ has died to go down to the pit, without advancing our skirmish lines and trying, by a double-quick movement, to snatch them as brands from the fire.

Oh that we may be, more than ever in the past, a revival church; a light to all around us, as the city that is set on a hill, which cannot be hid. Where other churches fail we must succeed. What they are unable to do, we must by God's grace accomplish. For this we were raised up: for this we have been preserved and made strong, and in this work we must go forth crying,

> "Lord revive us! Lord revive us!
> All our help must come from thee."

In all the allusions I have made to the work of the Lord under my own feeble labors, I hope none will attribute to me a spirit of vain-glory—such allusions had to come in naturally, in the narrative of my life, and will be to many, as well as to myself, in reading them, like green spots in the desert, and wells of water in a thirsty land.

I cannot close this account of my experience in the ministry without some personal remarks, which those to whom I may refer will please pardon me for making. I was, as the kind reader will recollect, early compelled to commence the struggle with this rough and rugged world, and literally to pioneer my own pathway up to manhood.

The truest friends I ever found, have been those in the traveling and local Ministry within the bounds of the Philadelphia Conference. I could easily record a long list of names on this page, that are cherished in my heart, and to whom for special attentions I am indebted, more deeply than I can express, or ever hope to repay.

The Rev. James Riddle, of Wilmington, Delaware, who has always shown himself a true and timely friend of young men, entering, and in the ministry, has from the hour I was converted until this day, never ceased to evince for me the generous and noble kindness of his warm Irish heart. The only way I can imagine, in which to reciprocate such disinterested friendship, is, to call upon him, whenever I have a favor to ask, and never fear to tax his kindness too far.

In regard to my present prospects: I feel that God is good to me, and his presence is with me in the way to heaven. My sincere desire is, to serve God and the Church of my choice more faithfully in the future. I ask an interest in the prayers of the Christian reader—

that I may be kept "steadfast, unmoveable, always abounding in the work of the Lord, and that my labor may not be in vain in the Lord."

When I sometimes retrospect my past life and mark the particular providences of God in my behalf, I am led to adopt the language of the beautiful hymn, and ask:

"When all thy mercies, O my God,
My rising soul surveys;
Transported with the view, I'm lost,
In wonder, love and praise."

Truly he has led me in a way I have not known;—in perils, privations, and danger; and has been ever ready to shield me from sudden and violent death.

I remember, when quite a small boy, once bathing in a certain river. The current was strong, and carried me out in deep water. As I could not swim, I was sinking to a watery grave, when a gentleman rescued me. This made a deep impression on my mind at the time, and so vivid is my realization of the interposition of Providence—that the event seems but as yesterday.

Once, while skating, on the same river, all alone, I was warned to get off, as the ice was moving rapidly beneath my feet towards the falls some distance below. When I looked at the situation, it was appalling. The ice had become detached from the shore, and was careering down with the force of the flood. I have heard it said that there were times when a person's hair has been known to stand up straight on their head through fright. Well, if ever my hair stood up straight upon my head, that was the time. I was compelled to spring into the deep and rapid current, and struggle for my life, among the broken fragments of ice, several pieces of which passed over me as I tried to reach the shore, which I did at length, through a merciful and kind Providence.

I also remember being thrown twice from a horse, each time the horse falling on me. An Indian pony once kicked me in the face, and I have known persons to be maimed, or even lose their life from a less cause.

While crossing the Alleghany Mountains when a boy, I put up at a hotel, and about midnight a robber and murderer entered my room. I was again the child of Providence, and to God I give the praise for my deliverance on that occasion. On another occasion in 1855, danger and death appeared imminent. I was attacked by three robbers a few miles east of Bedford, Pa., while traveling on horseback. During my itinerancy, I have often experienced the watch-care of one who is nigh at hand to help and save. When thrown from my carriage twice with great violence, I was graciously preserved without harm.

And, that the bullet has sped by me, or the shell and shot has not been allowed to molest or make me afraid; that I live to-day, rejoicing in my beloved country's triumph, and with a heart to thank God for all his goodness to me, is all through his unmerited grace.

Whatever may be my future course, I can say in the

words of the Psalmist: "My heart is fixed, O God, my heart is fixed; I will sing and give praise."

"This, this is the God I adore,
  My faithful unchangeable friend,
Whose love is as great as his power,
  And neither knows measure nor end.
'Tis Jesus the first and the last,
  Whose Spirit shall guide me safe home.
I'll praise Him for all that is past,
  And trust Him for all that's to come."

Soldier's Life.

Life in the Army, p. 69.

ARMY OF THE POTOMAC.

CHAPTER IX.

MUSTERING.

THE GREAT UPRISING OF THE NORTH—A PATRIOT'S DUTY—ORGANIZATION OF THE ONE HUNDRED AND TWENTY-SEVENTH REGIMENT—MARCHING ORDERS—WASHINGTON, D. C.—ACROSS THE POTOMAC—FORT "ETHAN ALLEN"—SECOND BULL RUN BATTLE—ANTIETAM—OUR YOUNG COLONEL—THE "CHRISTIAN BODY"—ORDERED TO JOIN THE ARMY OF THE POTOMAC—HEAVY MARCH—AMUSING SCENES—A SPLENDID SHOT—SCIENTIFIC PORK-BUTCHERING—DISAPPEARANCE OF A RAIL FENCE—A FRIGHTENED CITIZEN—THE "ELEVENTH MAINE"—THE CHAPLAIN BAMBOOZLED—MILITARY NECESSITY—ACQUIA CREEK—COMFORTLESS QUARTERS—GEN. BURNSIDE'S ARMY—CAMP ALLEMAN—MAJOR-GENERALS COUCH AND HOWARD.

WITH the great uprising of the northern people on account of the firing on our time-honored flag, I was drawn into hearty and active sympathy. When it became evident that secessionists, in their blind infatuation and rage, were determined on war, every true man was bound to show his colors. It thrilled my soul to hear of the great heart of the people being filled and fired with patriotic ardor. The stirring sound of fife and drum, the hurried movement of troops, the formation of camps, and the rapidity with which an army was collected, equipped, and placed around the Capital, gave ample evidence, that the Union was dear to the great masses, and would not be surrendered without a struggle to maintain the right against despotism.

I entered into the glorious cause without a question as to my duty, and assisted to the extent of my influence in recruiting companies for the war. I felt that I owed everything to my government in the struggle pending, until victory should crown her efforts in the suppression of the rebellion, and the external overthrow of its prime moving cause, slavery.

The One Hundred and Twenty-seventh Regiment Pennsylvania Volunteers was organized at Camp Curtin, on the 16th day of August, 1862, and left Harrisburg for Washington on the following morning. I have already intimated my connection with this body of troops as regularly commissioned Chaplain. We reached Washington, D. C., on the same day, crossed the Potomac into Virginia, and went into camp, which we named "Jennings," in honor of our Colonel. We remained here only a short time, under General Whipple, and were ordered to "Fort Ethan Allen," where we remained on guard duty during the second battle of "Bull Run." We could hear occasionally the roar of rebel cannon in the distance, and the sensation was peculiar for the first time. We next received orders to go into camp, and called it "Camp Boas," in honor of Colonel Boas, of Harrisburg.

Our duty here was to guard the Chain Bridge and picket duty in the defences of Washington. During the battle of Antietam we were under command of General Abercrombie, and spent two months at this post.

Here we held regular religious meetings, and spent the time very agreeably in such amusement as the soldier needs to while away the time. A company of men numbering about one thousand, will, if idle, invent many ways to have fun, and break the monotony of what would be a very dull mode of life.

Our youthful colonel displayed qualities which constitute the true soldier. He was kind to his command, but a strict disciplinarian, and won the respect and confidence of both officers and men.

Our next move was about three miles toward the front, where we formed a camp, and called it "Jennings," in honor of our Colonel. In this location we remained but three days, when we were ordered to our former post, near "Fort Ethan Allen." Here we established Camp "Dauphin," in honor of the native county of three-fourths of the men of our noble regiment. We were formed into a brigade, of which our Colonel was placed in command, leaving the charge of the regiment in the hands of Lieutenant-Colonel Alleman.

While in Camp Dauphin I formed an association embracing all the professors of religion, which we termed a "Christian body." This afterwards proved a great blessing to the men of our regiment. Our meetings were kept up with interest, and were largely attended.

On Sabbath, the 30th of November, much to our surprise, as quite a number of the officers had erected winter quarters, we received orders to be ready to march on the following morning to join the Army of the Potomac, then encamped near Fredericksburg, Va. Accordingly, on the morning of the 1st of December, 1862, we fell in, and took up the line of march during a heavy rain storm. Our route was through Washington, and down the north side of the Potomac to Acquia Creek.

The first day's march was very severe on the men, many of whom became exhausted with fatigue. I tried to relieve the most weary, by allowing them by turns to ride my horse, while I shouldered their muskets, and kept step to the music of the Union.

We passed through several counties of Maryland, where nearly all the inhabitants appear to be strong secessionists; and from their manner it was evident their sympathies all turned in favor of Jeff. Davis. The soldiers, knowing this, did not spare the poultry yards, as they passed along. I witnessed, one day, a very remarkable specimen of skill on the part of one of our privates, who, seeing two chickens in a barn-yard standing directly in line, raised his gun, and with a minie ball cut both their heads off. The trophy was soon slung over his shoulder, and he jogged on with the prospect of a good supper, and the applause of his companions, for being the best marksman in the ranks. Another man, taking it into his head to have a steak of fresh pork, boldly charged on, and captured a pig, which I saw him afterwards tie up to a tree, and with all the de-

Buckstown Camp Meeting.

Life in the Army, p. 73.

liberation and skill of a scientific butcher, proceed to dress, to the amusement of all who witnessed the transaction.

One evening as we had halted, and were arranging our camp for the night, with the aid of my servant boy Dick, I constructed my tent with one end supported by a rail fence; but as a military necessity, the men of the brigade very soon appropriated every rail of that fence to cook their coffee, and as a consequence, down came my tent, flat upon the ground. "Well," said I to Dick, "it is too late now to build another, let us look for lodging at that farm-house," which stood near by.

As we reached the place, a farmer who lived about a mile distant made his appearance, very much frightened and excited. He enquired for the commander, saying that the soldiers were killing his cattle and hogs, and that they threatened to shoot him if he interfered with them. I directed him to the Brigade Head-quarters, but the boys, supposing him to be a rebel, pointed out the wrong man, and the poor fellow became bewildered, and soon returned to me, exclaiming, "My God, I do not know what to do." I then inquired if he was a Union man. He answered that he was. "Well," said I, "if you will furnish me with supper and a good bed, and breakfast in the morning, I will go home with you and act as your guard." To this he agreed, and we were soon at his house. As I sat by the fire, the farmer looked down the lane and cried out to me in a very nervous way, "Yonder they come." "Keep cool," said I, "and I will manage the soldiers." So I waited until they approached so near that I heard voices in the hen-roost. I then went out and said, "Good evening, men." They stopped proceedings on finding me there, and I told them I hoped they would not take anything, for the owner said he was a good Union man, and he had already suffered to the amount of eight hogs. "Well," said the soldiers, "if he is a Union man we will not disturb his poultry, but it is a principle with us to pitch into the live stock of all secessionists, and set it down to the credit of Uncle Sam." I inquired to what regiment they belonged, and they answered, "The Eleventh Maine," and took their departure. The cream of the joke was, that they all belonged to my own regiment. But they put on so many airs, that I did not know a mother's son of them. I enjoyed a good night's rest and an excellent supper and breakfast, and this, after a weary march, was very refreshing. My Union friend presented me, in addition to the contract, with two well dressed chickens, and two pounds of butter, to regale myself with as we journeyed on. Thus ended my first and last guard duty.

There were quite a number of amusing circumstances, which transpired on this march, and which I have not here space to give in detail.

All along the route, secesh chickens, hogs, geese, ducks, turkeys, horses, mules, &c., were missing about their accustomed homes, and I suppose the citizens either put it down to military necessity, or made up their losses by blockade running.

We reached the Bay or River opposite Acquia Creek, on the 4th of December, and crossed over to the Virginia side, in rain and snow. The men suffered a great deal, having no dry place to lay their heads during that stormy night.

December 8th, we again took up our line of march and arrived within the lines of the Army of the Potomac on the afternoon of the 9th. We went into camp, which we named "Camp Alleman," in honor of our Lieutenant-Colonel, and here we had a little rest after our march of eight days. The officers and men stood the fatigue remarkably well, and proved themselves good soldiers. Our regiment was then placed in the second army corps, under Major-General Couch, and Major-General Howard, as Division Commander.

This began to look like war, in earnest, and the mighty army, of which we now formed an integral part, seemed to be impressed with the idea that serious business was near at hand. Awaiting the deliberations of the master minds, who were in war counsel, and correspondence with Washington, these tens of thousands were ready, at a word, to advance and meet the enemy. The chaplains were all industriously engaged, meetings were held, and the mails collected and conveyed a large number of letters from our men to their friends at home.

CHAPTER X.

WAR.

CAMP BROKEN—MARCH TO THE FRONT—FREDERICKSBURG—PREPARATIONS FOR BATTLE—RELIGIOUS MEETINGS—OPENING OF THE FIGHT—TERRIFIC CANNONADE—PONTOONS—REBEL SHARP-SHOOTERS ROUTED—A DARING EXPLOIT—CAPTAIN FOX MORTALLY WOUNDED—OUR REGIMENT ORDERED ACROSS—UNDER FIRE—CASUALTIES—THE REBEL YELL—THREE DAYS' TERRIBLE SLAUGHTER—DEFEAT OF OUR ARMY—CAUSES—RETREAT TO OUR OLD CAMP—"TRY, TRY AGAIN."

On December 10th, 1862, our camp was thrown into a state of unusual excitement, by orders received that we must prepare to move on the 11th. Our prayer and experience meetings on that evening were well attended, and deep seriousness seemed to fall upon the hearts of all. The men knew that they were now near the foe, and that a desperate battle was impending. Thoughts of home, and the many friends they had left behind; thoughts of the future,—the numerous risks of the battle-field, the probability, nay, the almost certainty, of some of the present company falling—all combined to bring a crowd of solemn reflections to every mind. We had a good meeting, and many expressed the hope, through Jesus, if no more permitted on earth to mingle our songs and supplications, that we should have a glorious meeting in the land of everlasting rest.

According to previous notice, the morning of the 11th found us early astir. The roll of drums, and the hurried formation of ranks of armed men, with the evolutions of artillery getting into position, produced a scene of bewildering confusion, while occasionally the startling sound of cannon broke upon the ear, and quickened the blood coursing in our veins. By six o'clock, A. M., the whole army was in motion, and ready for the command "forward," to the field of carnage and blood. It was a thrilling spectacle to see the thousands of officers and men, all obedient to one governing mind, wheel into their positions, and move away from their pleasant quarters, to try once more the issue of battle.

The Army of the Potomac was at this time in splendid condition, and capable of great achievements for their country and its glorious flag. Mingling with the enthusiasm of the movement, there could be observed a spirit of intense seriousness among the men. Many requested an interest in our prayers, and on every countenance could be plainly read the feelings of the heart, which were to conquer or die.

Our section of the army was halted at the Lacy House, just in front of the city of Fredericksburg.

We found the engineers busily engaged in laying pontoon-bridges across the river. This was a hazardous undertaking, and cost many a noble life. Again and again was the work interrupted by a murderous fire, kept up by rebel sharp-shooters on the other side: but, just as often, our brave fellows dashed on, and at length completed their task about three o'clock in the afternoon.

During this time, besides the sharp firing of musketry which was constantly kept up, about seventy-five of our cannon, which had been ranged on the heights, were belching forth their thunder, and raining desolation on the city, and rebel works around it.

A brave band of men volunteered, and crossed the river in a boat, to silence the rebel sharp-shooters. They were watched by thousands of eager eyes, as, amid the storm of bullets now directed on themselves, they landed and quickly stormed the rifle-pits, with such boldness and determination, that the sculking murderers either ran or surrendered.

One of that number was a private of Company I of our regiment, and few exploits of the war have evinced more true heroism than this expedition.

The bridges being now in order for the passage of troops, while our heavy ordnance was making the ground to tremble beneath our feet, and amid the yelling, cheering, and the wildest excitement, there was a dash made to cross the Rappahanock, and support our brave pioneers who held their ground on the opposite side. We could hear their shouts, and very soon they had reinforcements, which enabled them to advance and take possession of the city.

Quite a large number of our men were killed and wounded while engaged in laying the pontoon bridges, and among the slain of that heroic few who first crossed, was the noble Chaplain Fuller, of Massachusetts, killed, it is said, by a minie bullet, and that fired by a rebel woman.

Our brigade was the first column of troops ordered to the other side, and our regiment was the third in the order of crossing.

The enemy, of course, directed his fire on the bridge while crowded with our troops. Shot and shell came hurtling fast and furious on their devoted heads. Captain Fox, a gentlemanly, intelligent, and Christian soldier of our regiment was mortally wounded, by a fragment of shell, and died in a couple of hours. I performed the melancholy duty of assisting to bury his body the next day, under rebel artillery fire. Our Colonel was a target for the foe, and was fired at, but led the One Hundred and Twenty-seventh bravely on regardless of danger, until he entered the city, about half of which was occupied by our forces that night, and the balance next morning.

December 13th, the battle commenced in earnest, in the rear of the city, and also on our left, where General Franklin, having crossed below, engaged the enemy. Our regiment was ordered into the fight at about one o'clock, P. M., and remained in an exposed situation for several hours. A galling fire of rebel infantry and artillery, from concealed points, swept through their ranks, until they fell back under cover.

During this first day's engagement, Colonel Jennings was severely wounded in two places, but, like a brave man, he refused to leave the head of his regiment. Captains Henderson and Ball, and also Lieutenants Henry and Orth were wounded. Lieutenant Shoemaker was killed. He was a man of intelligence and courage. A number of other officers were injured, and several of our men were killed and wounded. I regret having no correct list of their names to insert here, as their bravery entitles them to the most honorable record posterity can bestow.

December 15th, our regiment was again under fire, Lieut.-Colonel Alleman commanding. The exposure and carnage was even greater than on the previous day. The Lieutenant-Colonel, Lieutenant Novinger, and several of the men were wounded, and our list of killed was considerable. In the three days' fighting our regiment lost, in killed, wounded, and missing, about one hundred and seventy-five officers and men.

I was near enough at times to the rebel lines during these three terrible days, to hear their unearthly, fiendish yell, such as no other troops or civilized beings ever uttered. It was not a hearty cheer, or hurrah, or roar, but a kind of shriek as dissonant as the "Indian war-whoop," and more terrible.

Major-General Franklin's Division on our left succeeded in capturing seven hundred prisoners, and in driving the rebel forces some distance at one time during the battle.

During the night of the 15th, the whole army retreated back across the river, without gaining any material advantage, and after having lost immense numbers of the bravest and best men in our ranks.

Why were we defeated? In my judgment it was, first, because the rebel army had had every advantage over us. They fought behind stone walls, and had natural intrenchments which made their position a very strong one, while our men were compelled to attack them and fight in an open field.

Secondly. I fear there was a great lack among our general officers of that concert of opinion and action which was necessary to success. *Jealousy* and *disloyalty* had much to do with the defeat of our noble army before Fredericksburg.

The commanding general, I think, should not be charged with this disaster. Great injustice has been done General Burnside, by placing the entire responsibility on his shoulders. He is a skilful commander, a brave soldier, and a high-minded Christian gentleman.

The sum total of our losses in the three days' fight, is reported at fifteen thousand men, which estimate includes the killed, wounded, missing, and prisoners, who fell into the hands of the enemy.

It is no wonder that both officers and men of the Army of the Potomac should feel dispirited as they fell back to their old camps again, after such a fearful sacrifice of life and limb. But still there was a determination to "pick flint" and try again. That secesh rag must be humbled to the dust. Those haughty rebels must come to grief. This gigantic rebellion *must* be put down, and the Union must and *shall* be preserved. Such a determination could easily be read in every face.

CHAPTER XI.

WINTER IN CAMP.

AFTER THE GREAT BATTLE—MUSIC IN CAMP—CHEERFULNESS RETURNS—REVIEW BY GEN. SUMNER—KIND WORDS TO THE CHAPLAIN—WHISKY RATIONS—FUN IN CAMP—SNOW-BALLS IN PLACE OF "MINIES"—AN INSULTED F. F. V.—THE LITTLE DRUMMER—ST. PATRICK'S DAY—DEVOTION SUCCEEDED BY DRUNKENNESS—HORSE RACING—EXHORTATION BY MAJOR-GENERAL HOWARD—SALE OF LIQUOR STOPPED—GAMBLERS RIDING ON A RAIL—RELIGIOUS MEETINGS—REVIVAL, AND NUMBERS CONVERTED.

CHEERFULNESS soon began to prevail, and the gloom consequent on our discomfiture at Fredericksburg, was dispelled by the hope of future success.

The officers and men of our regiment, finding they had to make the best of their present quarters for the winter, displayed their ingenuity in ways and means to pass the time as comfortably as possible. Our excellent regimental band did much toward reviving, and keeping up the spirits of the men. The power of martial music is wonderful, and we all felt indebted to the musicians for their unwearied efforts to amuse and cheer us, and to Mr. Ball, the efficient leader, and all the members of our late band, we owe a thousand thanks, for their assistance in our religious meetings, by discoursing sacred music so frequently.

While Major-General Sumner was reviewing the right grand division of the Army of the Potomac one day, I was standing in my proper position as a staff officer of the regiment, and he rode up, accompanied by a dashing staff, and stopping where I was, inquired very kindly if I was Chaplain. I answered that I was. He then inquired if any of the officers opposed me, and if I visited the hospitals. I informed him that I visited the hospitals twice a day, and received no opposition to my work from any one. He then said, "Chaplain, if any of them interferes with you in the future, let me know his name and rank." I thanked the Major-General very sincerely, and told him that was the style I liked, and would certainly report to him, if any shoulder-strapped gentleman crossed my way in the performance of my duties. The General then put spurs to his charger, and passed on to review the troops.

Such an act of kind consideration shown me, in this public manner, by the distinguished Sumner, gave me great encouragement, and exalted the General to a very elevated place in my esteem, as it evinced very plainly his decided countenance for good order, morality, and religion in the army, and his sympathy and friendship toward the often slighted, and much abused chaplain. If all other Major-Generals had followed his example toward a worthy and excellent body of men, as it was both their duty and interest to do, the act would have been more creditable, and the results more beneficial than was often the case.

That officer, I care not who he is, who gives his sanction, directly or indirectly, to profanity, vice, and immorality, is a disgrace to the service, and ought to be dismissed at once.

After General Hooker took command, an order was issued, allowing whisky rations to be distributed to the army. As soon as I became aware of this arrangement, I asked our Colonel if he was going to allow the issuing of whisky rations to the men of his command, remarking at the same time, that he had under his care the sons of many praying fathers and mothers, and that I thought this course would demoralize the men, and awaken in them such an appetite for strong drink as would be highly dangerous, and might lead some of them to ruin. The gallant and noble-minded Colonel informed me in an emphatic manner that there should not be *one drop* of whisky distributed among either officers or men of his regiment. I thanked him, and repaired quickly to my tent, where on my knees I gave glory and praise to God for having such a Colonel, and that he had a proper respect and care for the moral welfare of his command.

He differed very widely from many others of his grade in this particular. What a blessing it would have been if all had been actuated by the same principle.

As the dull, weary days of winter rolled on, the officers and men devised many a scheme of innocent fun and amusement in Camp Alleman. Snow-balling was one of the most popular and exciting pastimes resorted to. Sometimes our regiment and the Sixty-ninth New York, that was encamped very near us, would get up a regular pitched battle, and instead of the "minie," would try to demolish each other with volleys of snow-balls. At times the Sixty-ninth would bring out their time-honored and bullet-riddled battle-flag, and challenge our boys to try and capture it. Again our men would display their colors, and dare the others to come and take it. While the two regiments were engaged one day in a regular "set-to," a secesh citizen was riding past, and received a tremendous whack from a snow-ball which was thrown by one of the little drummer boys. The instant Mr. Secesh was hit, he jumped from his horse and ran towards the boy, as though he intended to knock him down. At that moment two of our men who were watching the movement stepped forward, and informed the Johnny Reb not to dare to lay the weight of his finger upon that little boy. So the insulted Virginian, concluding that discretion was the better part of valor, remounted his poor old steed, and rode on his way a wiser if not a better man.

While we lay in Camp Alleman, First Lieutenant Wm. R. Orth died. He was an exemplary young man, of amiable character, and was much respected and beloved for his many fine traits. Having lived as a Christian should, he departed with a hope bright and full of a blessed immortality.

Saint Patrick's day was a notable period in the army, especially among the Irish Catholics. The pious of this persuasion had a grand time of religious services in the morning, and this was quickly followed by a general spree. Drunkenness, horse-racing, and fist-fighting became the order—or rather the disorder of the afternoon, and the day closed in a regular "Tipperary" fashion.

I met Major-General Howard on one occasion, under circumstances that I shall never forget. This pure patriot, and brave soldier, is known to be a sincere Christian, and everywhere feels it to be both a privilege and duty to stand up for Jesus. The occasion I refer to was on a certain Sabbath. I was preaching to my men on the subject of the last judgment, and on concluding my sermon, learned that General Howard had been one of my hearers. I at once introduced him to the officers and soldiers who composed my congregation.

The General stepped up and addressed them, saying, "Officers and men of the One Hundred and Twenty-seventh Regiment, Pennsylvania Volunteers, I am glad to see so many of you out to hear preaching this Sabbath morning, and I would to God, that all the men of my command were true followers of Christ Jesus, the Lord. Soldiers, allow me to express, with your Chaplain, the sincere desire of my heart, that we may meet at the right hand of the Great Judge in that day, which he has described to us. Soldiers, may God bless you all."

That short address made a deep and lasting impression on our men, and caused them to think more highly of the General than ever before. He is not only a true friend, but an active and practical helper of the Chaplains, in their sacred calling in the army, and has been known to kneel by the side of the wounded and dying soldier, and tell him of Christ and salvation.

I was put in possession of the fact one day, that the Brigade Commissary was selling liquor to officers and men, by the canteen full, and determined at once to stop the traffic.

I rode down to General Howard's head-quarters, and made known my case. He promptly issued an order prohibiting it.

A few days afterwards some of the officers of the Brigade, and a certain officer of my own regiment, informed me that General Howard had ordered the Commissary not to sell them any more whisky. They, of course, knew nothing of my connection with this business, and did not dream that I was the cause of stopping their rum, at this particular time. If they but knew how much poisonous strychnine was probably in that stuff, they ought to have regarded any one as a benefactor and philanthropist who put forth exertions to stop the trade, and prevent the evil consequent on using it.

One Sabbath morning there were two Virginia gamblers who came into our camp, and induced some of the men to play cards with them. When Colonel Jennings heard of it, he sent a guard down to the spot where the gamblers had begun operations, and had the two "professionals" marched up in front of his tent. He then gave them a reprimand, and by his suggestion they were both honored with a ride upon a rail. In this he served the scamps exactly right, only, in my judgment, it would have set off the matter a little more effectually to have allowed them, and all their kin, a coat of tar and feathers before mounting them. This would have capped the climax, and made a good Sabbath sermon on the sin of gambling and its consequences.

Our "Christian body" continued to maintain its identity and efficiency. We had preaching every Sabbath when the weather would admit, an experience-meeting every Sabbath night, and prayer-meeting every night of the week in my tent. God honored the means employed, and blessed us with a gracious revival of religion in camp, which lasted several weeks, and resulted in the conversion of a number of souls.

We had many seasons of refreshing from the presence of the Lord, and it is a matter of joy to me that many of our men returned home from the service of their country better than when they enlisted. It is my prayer that they all may be made partakers of saving grace, become valiant soldiers of Jesus, and when discharged on earth, that they may live forever in the kingdom of God.

8*

CHAPTER XII.

HOOKER'S CAMPAIGN.

HOOKER'S CAMPAIGN—THE CONDITION OF THE ARMY—THE TROOPS IN MOTION—CROSSING OF THE RAPPAHANNOCK—PRAYER BEFORE BATTLE—AN EVENTFUL SABBATH—REFLECTIONS—CAPTURE OF THE "HEIGHTS"—EVENING SERMON IN FREDERICKSBURG—THE ARMY VICTORIOUS—A STRANGE TIME TO RETREAT—KILLED, WOUNDED, AND MISSING—WHERE THE BLAME LIES—THE FINAL DEFEAT OF WHISKY—OUR OFFICERS TRUE TO TEMPERANCE—TERM OF SERVICE EXPIRED—ORDERED TO REPORT AT HARRISBURG—HOMEWARD BOUND—GRAND RECEPTION—GALA DAY—CONCLUSION.

ON the 1st of May, 1863, we again find the army in fine condition. Major-General Hooker having been placed in command, brought every arm of the service up to the highest degree of efficiency for the opening campaign. At this date, we had been in Camp Alleman for five months, when the order came to prepare for a forward movement. On the 2d of May the whole army was in motion, and a battle impending. The main body crossed the Rappahannock at "United States Ford," while Sedgwick's Corps crossed below the City of Fredericksburg. The advance was soon engaged with the enemy, who, aware of our intentions, was determined to contest our progress every foot of the way. Being on the eve of battle, I was much exercised in prayer for myself, the regiment, and our whole army.

I believe God heard my prayer, for I felt composed during the excitement incident to the terrific engagements which ensued. Often in the very path of danger, and with death and destruction all around, I felt secure in the confidence of my heavenly Father's protection and care.

On Sabbath morning, the 3d of May, instead of wending my quiet way to the house of God, or engaging in divine service in the field, the exigencies of another sanguinary battle demanded all my attention.

I cannot in these pages attempt any description of military evolutions, or account for consequences, by telling how "fields were lost or won." My business was to cheer the faint, to succor the weary and wounded, and to minister to the wants of those dying on the cold ground or in our temporary hospitals, far from friends and home. The heights of Fredericksburg on that memorable Sabbath presented a scene of activity and terror far beyond my powers of description. The noise of battle rolled on, the belching flame, and heavy clouds of smoke, the din and dreadful strife between contending hosts, all combined to make an impression on my feelings in contrast with the memories of home, and the fact that whilst tens of thousands of my fellow-citizens were being summoned by the sweet tone of the church-going bell, to pray and offer praise peacefully to God, thousands here were dying for the right, for the cause of God, humanity, and constitutional liberty.

After several hours of hard fighting, Sedgwick's corps on the right, assisted by our division on the left, succeeded in capturing the famous heights of Fredericksburg.

Twelve pieces of artillery and four hundred prisoners fell into our hands. I never left the field all that day of sorrow and pain.

The battle closed late in the afternoon, with our forces in possession of the city and its surroundings. As our regiment was ordered back to the city to do guard duty, I gathered a congregation of soldiers, including a few of the citizens, and preached in one of the Methodist churches at night, under circumstances of extraordinary interest.

What a Sabbath day's work this was to me! I only hope that some good was done that eternity alone will disclose. It was really one of the most eventful days of my past life, and I am glad to testify that I was not left without the comforting presence of God.

The chaplains, as a general thing, displayed true Christian courage, and a commendable zeal in the performance of their duties.

At the post of danger, wherever their respective regiments were called to stand, there these men of God were ready to point the dying soldier to Christ the Saviour of the world, and by needful attention to the wounded, to save valuable lives.

No remark is more true than that made by General Howard, and it does honor to both his head and heart, "The faithful chaplain is *the* man of the regiment."

While in our position on the 5th of May, and confident of success, an order was issued to fall back, and the whole army retreated to the north side of the Rappahanock River. The casualties to our regiment, in the late battle, indicate how close we were to the work of death, and how bravely our officers and men pressed forward in the fight. Lieutenant Kinsley was wounded severely, and died soon afterwards. He was a gentlemanly young man, and a fine soldier. Lieutenant-Colonel Alleman was struck with a piece of shell, knocked from his horse, and severely injured. Sergeant Hummel was struck in the forehead with a fragment of shell, and died from the effects of his wounds in a few days. The sergeant was a native of Harrisburg, and was a very fine young man.

A number of others were killed or wounded, making the entire loss of our regiment, in the two great battles under Burnside and Hooker, two hundred and twenty. The loss of our army in the recent battle, including killed, wounded, and missing, with those taken prisoners by the enemy, was eight thousand.

It was unaccountable to me then, and is so to this day to many of the officers, why we were ordered to retreat. Certainly "Fighting Joe" and the brave army who followed him were not defeated. The rebels admit an immense loss; and we had large numbers of reserve troops who were not in action; but waiting and ready to be ordered to advance. There was no sign or feeling of defeat among our forces. The troops came out of battle in good spirits, full of vigor and hope, and all ready, at a moment's notice, to move forward again. To say at that time, in the presence of any of our officers or men, that we had been whipped, would have been resented as an insult. These considerations, all taken together, prove conclusively that, whatever induced the commander to relinquish his position on the very eve of a signal victory, it could not be the fact of disaster. It must have been the apprehension of defeat.

Soon after these occurrences I had another difficulty on the whisky question. An order was issued from head-quarters that the entire army should be regularly supplied with whisky rations. When the order came to our regiment Colonel Jennings happened to be field-officer of the day, and Lieutenant-Colonel Alleman was in command of the regiment. I was not in camp at the time; but, thank God, our Lieutenant-Colonel sent word down to head-quarters that he could not allow the distribution of whisky under any circumstances to our men. They then sent up a second order, and he firmly persisted in his refusal to allow it. He was then politely requested to appear at head-quarters, and, just as he was about to start, I returned to camp. He informed me of the whole affair, remarking that he supposed they would take his sword. "Well," said I to him, "you stand firm as a rock, and do not take a word back. Let them take your sword. Our term of service has expired; and if they dare to take it for doing your duty I will publish the whole matter; and the men of our regiment intend to present you with a better sword as soon as we reach Harrisburg." The Lieutenant-Colonel did stand "firm as a rock," and they did not take his sword. We carried the day, and from first to last did not allow our men to be poisoned with their abominable "whisky rations."

Both Colonel Jennings, and Lieutenant-Colonel Alleman of the One hundred and twenty-seventh Pennsylvania Volunteers, deserve the gratitude of all friends of morality and temperance, for their uncompromising opposition to this curse of humanity. For all sensible men must admit that drunkenness, and everything that leads to it, in the army and elsewhere, has been productive of "evil, and only evil, and that continually."

Those who have been conversant with the facts, know that abundance of liquor has always been smuggled into our armies by the connivance of high officials, and that officers of superior grade have frequently imbibed too much, thereby rendering them unfit to command our brave patriotic men; and that intemperance has wrought disaster, and caused blunders, and mistakes on many a bloody field.

Yes, in some instances, where there was no other ostensible cause for retreats and defeats, the whisky bottle may be set down as the worker of immense mischief. I care not how great the general may be, or how skilful to command an army, when his brains become addled by too much "Jersey lightning," he is not fit to drive a decent mule team, much less plan and direct an important campaign.

Sobriety, and a cool clear head, is just as necessary to our Generals, Colonels, Captains, and Lieutenants, who have the management of men, as military science; and indeed the one will not avail much, without the other. Many of the privates of our large armies, have been an example in this respect to their superior officers, and have passed successively through various ordeals without being either drunk, or addicted to the use, in any form, or to any extent, of intoxicating liquor.

On the 13th of May, 1863, our term of service having expired, we received orders to report at Harrisburg. Consequently we left for Acquia Creek, and secured transportation for our destination, where, without further mishap, we in due time arrived on the morning of the 16th. Our return had been expected, and the brave One hundred and twenty-seventh, with its noble officers, bearing, many of them, their honorable scars, met with a cordial and enthusiastic welcome home.

That day will long live in our memory. The Governor, heads of the various departments, crowds of citizens of the city and surrounding country, ladies with bright smiles and waving banners, the resounding hurrah! and all the associations of our generous reception, was a fitting and full reward for what we had endured in weary marches, and braved on bloody battle-fields, in the performance of that high duty, for which we had given ourselves to the service of our beloved country.

Many towns and cities have done well in furnishing men and means for the war, and have extended kindly greetings to the returning soldier, but in these respects, none has exceeded Harrisburg, the Capital of our glorious and patriotic Commonwealth. Her sons and fair daughters are an honor to the Keystone State, and in behalf of the One Hundred and Twenty-seventh, I take the liberty here to express my most sincere and fervent thanks for our grand reception, and such a recognition of our services as was then and there publicly given us.

Thus ended my experiences of army life in camp and field. I shall next try to recount my views in other departments of the service, if the kind reader will follow the lines of my hurried pen.

9

CHAPTER XIII.

THE ONE HUNDRED AND TWENTY-SEVENTH PENNSYLVANIA VOLUNTEERS.

DISTINGUISHING CHARACTERISTICS OF THE OFFICERS AND PRIVATES OF THE ONE HUNDRED AND TWENTY-SEVENTH REGIMENT PENNSYLVANIA VOLUNTEERS—FIELD OFFICERS—COLONEL W. W. JENNINGS—PEN AND INK SKETCHES—TESTIMONIAL BY THE OFFICERS—COLONEL JENNINGS, JUNIOR—LIEUTENANT-COLONEL ALLEMAN—A WORKING OFFICER—HANDSOME PRESENT—THE LIEUTENANT-COLONEL IN PURSUIT OF A REBEL SPY—SOLD—THE SPY A WOMAN—HINT TO THE LADIES—MAJOR ROHRER—SURGEON E. H. HORNER—STAFF OFFICERS—ASSISTANT SURGEON H. L. VASTINE—CHAPLAIN J. CHANDLER GREGG—QUARTERMASTER JOHN F. ORTH—ADJUTANT A. C. CHAYNE—LINE OFFICERS—CAPTAIN J. WESLEY AWL, &c., &c—LIEUTENANTS, AND THEIR RESIDENCES—PRIVATES—A RESPECTABLE BODY—GOOD MORALS—TABLE, SHOWING WHERE RECRUITED—THE CHAPLAIN'S FAREWELL.

FIELD OFFICERS. Colonel W. W. Jennings, who commanded the One Hundred and Twenty-seventh Pennsylvania Regiment, is a young man of good judgment, rather quiet in his disposition, of few words, decided in his opinions, of steady and temperate habits, and possessing a kind heart; always making a true friend, as there is nothing hidden or deceitful to be found in his noble nature; always ready and willing to listen to the complaint of the private soldier, and extend to him his sympathy and protection. He possessed those peculiar characteristics which at once distinguish a model man.

While on duty he was *Colonel* Jennings; but off duty he caused all to feel easy and at home in his presence. Recognizing in each a fellow-soldier, he never gave evidence that he considered himself a superior. It was this particular feature in his character which rendered him so popular with the men of his command. He is calm and self-possessed, and as a general thing free from excitement. He is very plain in his dress, entirely free from those manifestations of vanity that stand out so prominently in the character of many of our military officers. The time spent by many in combing, brushing and dressing, our Colonel spent in studying military tactics, reading, and conversation; or enjoying innocent fun with his clerk. Whenever you would see a large pipe made out of the root of a tree, with a stem about two feet long, moving about through camp, you might expect to see the Colonel in its rear. When this machine was fired up, you might see great clouds of smoke rolling upward like the mists of morning. The pipe, in camp, was his intimate friend and companion. The Colonel fared sumptuously every day. He was very careful to see that the wants of his inner man were supplied with provisions of the best quality that the market and circumstances afforded, without consulting expense. He is a young man of industrious habits, but was not the earliest riser in camp, and seemed confident that the sun would rise regularly whether he did or not. If he will excuse me I may inform his friends that many of us were accustomed to think we had the *best-looking* Colonel in the Army of the Potomac. He is an excellent singer, and had his training in the choir of the Locust Street M. E. Church in the city of Harrisburg, before joining the army; and I might add, that his very worthy parents have been members of that church for a number of years. The fact that he was rocked in the cradle of Methodism, and educated under Methodist influences, is one of the great causes why he stands to-day a true and upright man.

He seems to have been blessed with natural military abilities, as is proven by the fact that the commanding generals under whom our regiment was placed, manifested a great interest in him. They discovered that he had the qualities of a true soldier centered in him; hence he was often placed in command of brigades, over colonels older than himself both in years and experience. He was always kind to me, attended public preaching, and encouraged others to do so. He was brave in battle; for although severely wounded in the early part of the first engagement, he kept it concealed from his men, and remained in command until his regiment was ordered off the field; and the next day, while in the hospital in Fredericksburg, unfit for duty, at a time when there was every prospect of the rebels shelling the city, I tried in vain to convince him of the propriety of his being carried across the river, beyond the range of the enemy's cannon. He answered me, "Chaplain, I want to remain with the men of my regiment." I need scarcely add to this picture of his character, that he was very popular with the officers and privates of his regiment. At the close of our term of service, the commissioned officers presented him with a costly silver service as a token of our esteem. We also presented his little son, Colonel Jennings, Jr., with a beautiful silver memento, hoping at the same time that he might live to become as distinguished as his father.

Col. Jennings is a native and resident of Harrisburg, and is a citizen of whom that city may well be proud.

Lieutenant-Colonel H. C. Alleman is a young man of marked ability as a public speaker, and a lawyer of great energy, determination, and tireless industry. This has contributed greatly to his success in life as a public man. It matters very little what opposition may confront him, his indomitable will and untiring perseverance enable him to surmount it. He was truly the working man of our regiment, doing much of the public writing. He was always ready and willing to write for, or aid in any way possible, the officers or enlisted men of the regiment who might desire his services. He was not off duty one day during our term of service, except during sickness. He has an obliging, kind disposition; but is a man of strong prejudice, very emphatic in his language, and decided in his opinions. He was a strict disciplinarian, and a vegetarian in his diet, not even drinking coffee or tea at his meals. He never drinks intoxicating liquors of any kind, and may be considered a true friend of the cause of temperance. He proved himself to be an efficient and brave officer in each of the great battles. It will be remembered that during the last battle he was struck with a piece of shell and knocked off his horse. The colonel of the regiment requested me to convey him off the field, but he refused to go with me, saying he wished to remain with the regiment. He is very gay in his dress, and in that particular excelled any of our officers. He is a man that enjoys a good joke, and is full of fun, often seeing objects to laugh at that others would pass by unnoticed. He was very kind to me, and attended public preaching, encouraging others to do so. The privates of the regiment presented him with a very costly and handsome sword at the expiration of our term of service, as a token of their esteem. The following joke is told of him. One day while he and another officer were returning from battalion drill across the Chain Bridge, the guard informed him that a person whom they considered a spy, had just passed, dressed in woman's apparel: our lieutenant-colonel spurred his fine cream-colored steed, moving forward with his companion in hot pursuit, at the rate of two-forty on a plank road. They had concluded it would be a big thing to capture a spy: but lo and behold, the supposed spy turned out to be a lady, and she got beyond our lines before being captured by her pursuers! The colonel will excuse me if I inform the ladies of Harrisburg that although he failed to make a capture then, he is still continuing the pursuit. May he soon succeed in capturing, not a rebel female spy, but one of the fair daughters of the Keystone State as the future Mrs. H. C. Alleman, and may he realize that there is more pleasure in possession, than even in pursuit on horseback. He is also a resident of the city of Harrisburg.

Major J. Rohrer was a quiet, self-possessed man, kind and social, temperate in his habits, and decided in his opinions. He displayed good judgment, and proved himself to be a worthy, efficient, and brave officer, performing his duties with faithfulness and success. He made many friends among the private soldiers, by franking their letters, and other acts of kindness shown them. If the Major will pardon me, I might add that in the opinion of many he was considered a very fine-looking officer. Residence, Middletown, Pennsylvania.

STAFF OFFICERS. Surgeon E. H. Horner, by promotion, is a Christian gentleman of superior abilities as a medical man. He possesses an amiable disposition, and proved himself to be a very efficient officer. He attended public preaching, and gave me every possible encouragement in my daily visits to the hospital.

Assistant Surgeon H. S. Vastine was a young man of undoubted medical abilities, temperate in his habits, possessing a kind heart, very mischievous and full of fun, and very popular with the regiment. Residence, Cattawissa, Pennsylvania.

Chaplain, the reader's humble servant, John C. Gregg, of the Philadelphia Conference.

Quartermaster John F. Orth was a young man of energy and enterprise, and somewhat gay in his dress. When this tall young officer was riding upon his tall gray horse, he had a tall time of it, and they made a very tall appearance. When his fast steed was under full speed, it always reminded me of a thunder storm, with flashing lightning. He made an excellent officer. Residence, Hummelstown, Pennsylvania.

Adjutant A. C. Chayne is a young man of a good disposition, gentlemanly and Christian in his conduct, and of a fine soldierly appearance. He made a very good adjutant. This young officer was in the habit of exercising his vocal organs in such a musical style, that in passing his tent he often caused many of us to halt and listen with pleasure and delight to his melodious voice, and the charming vocal music he discoursed to our great edification. Residence, Harrisburg, Pennsylvania.

LINE OFFICERS. *Captains.* Captain J. Wesley Awl commanding Company B, is an intelligent, Christian young man, a good public speaker, an able lawyer, and a very efficient officer, possessing fine military abilities. He is a man of few words, of a very quiet disposition, of unassuming manners, and very plain in his dress.

He is the calmest and most self-possessed man that I ever met; entirely free from excitement in the hour of danger, never in a hurry, but always in time. The Captain displayed a great amount of coolness, self-possession, undaunted courage and bravery in each of the battles in which our regiment was engaged. He was very popular with the men of his company, although a strict disciplinarian. He assisted me in holding and sustaining my religious meetings, more than any other officer of the regiment. He stood by me as Chaplain only as a faithful Christian could, being ready at all times to assist and encourage by his influential presence the work of doing good among the men. I pronounce him a model young man, and think he deserves the sincere thanks of all the parents, sisters and brothers of the privates of our regiment, for the noble stand he took in favor of morality and religion during our term of service.

Were you to meet a man passing quietly about through camp, keenly, but unostentatiously observing everything occurring around him, with his pantaloons stuck inside his boots, a very broad-brimmed, low-crowned slouch hat on his head, stepping along with great solidity upon the heel of his boots, and the inevitable pipe in his mouth, you might very readily conclude him to be the original Captain J. W. Awl. I often visited him in his tent and always found him quietly enjoying himself, heels higher than his head, in reading or smoking. If the Captain will pardon me, I will say that in and out of his tent, in all his movements, he reminded me of a confirmed bachelor. Residence, Harrisburg, Pennsylvania.

Captain James Henderson, commanding Company C, is a kind, gentlemanly man, very intelligent, and an excellent medical officer. He took good care of the men of his company, and was very brave upon the battlefield; attended public preaching, and gave his influence in favor of others doing so. Residence, Hummelstown, Pennsylvania.

Captain James B. Keene, by promotion, commanding Company D, is a young man of religious habits, was a member of our Christian body, and a faithful and brave officer. He attended all my religious meetings. Residence, Harrisburg, Pennsylvania.

Captain L. L. Greenwalt, commanding Company E, is a man of very steady habits and entirely free from any exhibition of vanity in his dress. The captain is what many would call a rough and ready man, just the kind of men we need to command our armies. The many starched-up, kid glove, and band-box officers of our army, have proven to be a great nuisance, from a want of mind, heart, and preparation for the work of putting down the rebellion. We need rough and ready men to command, as well as in the ranks. I have often been amused at the manifestations of pride on the part of many of the officers of our army, and concluded that if *fine dress* and making a *great show* would conquer a peace, there has been enough of it exhibited to put down twenty rebellions. Captain Greenwalt is a Christian gentleman of large experience, having traveled through California and many other parts of the country. He was very popular with the men of his company, and made a very reliable, brave, and excellent officer. He was considered by many a very fine-looking man. He attended divine worship and assisted me in my work. His residence is Lebanon, Pennsylvania.

Captain Wm. H. H. Hummel, commanding Company F, is a young man of fine social qualities, and enjoyed the confidence of the men of his command. He was an excellent and brave officer, having performed his duties with fidelity and success. Residence, Harrisburg, Pennsylvania.

Captain John J. Ball, commanding Company G, is a very pleasant man and an excellent drill-master, always cheerful and full of fun. On Christmas day, while in camp, the captain prepared a Christmas tree that excited much laughter and fun. He had it trimmed off beautifully with old shoes, empty bottles, &c. He succeeded well in performing his duties, was brave in battle, and kind to his men. Residence, City of Harrisburg.

Captain John R. Shott commanding Company H, is a gentlemanly man, and commanded his company with ability and success. He was on detached duty the greater part of the time of service. His only son and only child, who was a member of his company, died during our term of service. This great loss almost broke the Captain's heart. Residence, Middletown, Pennsylvania.

Captain C. A. Nissley commanding Company I, by promotion, is a fine-looking, gentlemanly young man of soldierly bearing: an intelligent, brave, and efficient officer. Under his command, Company I improved in drill and appearance. He attended public preaching, and influenced others to do so. All I could say would be in the Captain's favor. Residence, Hummelstown, Pennsylvania.

Captain J. W. Dougherty, commanding Company K, by promotion, is a young man of intelligence, very lively in his disposition, and full of animation. He was very gay in his dress, always wearing a large feather in his hat, from which one would conclude that he was rather a fast young man; but I cannot admit the correctness of that conclusion. In one particular he was very much like our Colonel, that is, he was very fond of good living. This young Captain made a very efficient officer, and succeeded well in his work. If he will excuse me, I will say that the same remark I have heard made about Captains Greenwalt, Awl, Nissley and Keene, I have heard expressed in his case, namely, that the young ladies of the far-famed Keystone State ought to enter their solemn protest against either of them living any longer in the state of single blessedness. What say, you fair daughters of Pennsylvania? What say you, brother bachelors, in self-defence? Captain J. W. Dougherty resides in Lebanon, Pennsylvania.

LIEUTENANTS. The following are the names and address of the Lieutenants of the One hundred and twenty-seventh regiment Pennsylvania Volunteers.

First Lieut. A. J. Fager, Company B. Residence, Harrisburg, Pa.
Second Lieut. Wm. McCarroll, Company B. Residence, Harrisburg, Pa.
First Lieut. Charles D. Wise, Company C. Residence, Hummelstown, Pa.
Second Lieut. David Hummel, Company C. Residence, Hummelstown, Pa.
First Lieut. Charles Osborn, Company D. Residence, Luzerne Co., Pa.
Second Lieut. Marcus Novinger, Company D. Residence, Millersburg, Pa.
First Lieut. Wm. P. Carmony, Company E. Residence, Lebanon, Pa.
Second Lieut. J. A. Bowman, Company E. Residence, Lebanon, Pa.
First Lieut. John T. Morgan, Company F. Residence, Harrisburg, Pa.
Second Lieut. T. G. Sample, Company F. Residence, Harrisburg, Pa.
First Lieut. George Hynicka, Company G. Residence, Harrisburg, Pa.
Second Lieut. Hudson Denny, Company G. Residence, Luzerne Co., Pa.
First Lieut. Isaiah Willis, Company H. Residence, Middletown, Pa.
Second Lieut. Nizzley, Company H. Residence, Middletown, Pa.
First Lieut. Jerome W. Henry, Company I. Residence, Annville, Pa.
Second Lieut. Wm. W. Reed, Company I. Residence, Harrisburg, Pa.
First Lieut. D. S. Long, Company K. Residence, Lebanon, Pa.
Second Lieut. J. W. Barr, Company K. Residence, Schuylkill Co., Pa.

The Lieutenants above named were a very fine body of young men, gentlemanly in their conduct, brave in battle, and very efficient officers. They performed their duties with faithfulness and success. All I could say of them would be in their favor as a body. Many of them attended Divine worship.

The reader will perceive that I have spoken favorably of the officers of my late regiment. I have done so, because in my sincere judgment there never was a more worthy corps of officers placed in command of any regiment of men.

The following shows where the different companies of the regiment were recruited:

Company B in and around the City of Harrisburg, Pa.
Company C in and around Hummelstown, Pa.
Company D in and around Harrisburg, Pa.
Company E in and around Lebanon, Pa.
Company F in and around Harrisburg, Pa.
Company G in and around Harrisburg, Pa.
Company H in and around Middletown, Pa.
Company I in Lebanon and Adams Counties, Pa.
Company K in Lebanon and Schuylkill Counties, Pa.

In speaking of the privates of the One Hundred and Twenty-Seventh Regiment, Pennsylvania Volunteers, I am happy to be able to testify in their favor as a body. I would remark,

First, They were intelligent above the average, as is proven by the fact that in one company there were eleven school-teachers and three lawyers, and each of the others had quite a large proportion of very intelligent men.

Secondly, They were a noble-minded body of men, the most of whom were incapable of performing a mean act.

Thirdly, They were men of good moral character and respectability at home. Many of the best families of Dauphin, Lebanon, and Adams Counties were represented in our regiment.

Fourthly, They were temperate in their habits; for I never saw but three of their number under the influence of intoxicating liquors during our term of service. I desire all the cowardly sympathizers with armed rebellion, that remained at home to aid the rebels, to learn that they belie and slander the noble private soldiers of our army when they pronounce them a body of drunkards. I take great pleasure in informing the enemies of the private soldiers of our army that, if they wish to find drunkards, they may look at home, and they will find countless multitudes in civil life, and increase the number by including themselves. It is a well-known fact that the great majority of the enemies of our glorious cause at home, are those drunken, degraded wretches, that seldom, if ever, draw a sober breath. They, therefore, should cease to accuse the private soldier of that for which nine-tenths of them are not guilty.

Fifthly, They were brave in battle; having fought for their country and her cherished institutions with becoming manliness and courage.

Sixthly, Many of them were Christians, and united with us in our "Christian body" in camp. I would again inform the enemies of our soldiers at home that they slander the great multitudes of Christian men in our armies when they declare that none can live a Christian life when there. I assert that the men who say so could not live as Christians themselves, for lack of brains, courage, and decision of character. Many of the most pious men of the land were to be found in the army among the private soldiers; for, with many others of my regiment, I can testify that we never attended church so frequently, or served God so faithfully at home, as we did when far from home and friends. A common want of divine assistance drove us to the mercy-seat. I firmly believe that our soldiers in the army serve God more faithfully than many who make loud professions of Christianity at home.

At the close of our term of service I was unanimously recommended by the commissioned officers to the President for a re-appointment in the army as chaplain. They in this way testified to my efficiency, and manifested their appreciation of my labors.

I would inform my brother officers that I heard Colonel Jennings declare, a few moments before we were mustered out of service, that he had never seen cause to regret having made any of his appointments. This I consider a high compliment to all who obtained their appointments through his influence.

In conclusion, I would say to all the officers and privates of our regiment who may read this sketch, that I shall ever retain a kind regard for them, and, with the feelings of a friend, I would request all who are not Christians to give their hearts to Christ the Lord. To those who are followers of Christ I would say, Dear brethren in the Lord, as we had so many glorious religious meetings together while in camp in tents below, let us all live true to God, the Church, and each other, so that if we never all meet on earth, we may finally meet in heaven, to part no more. Officers and privates of my late regiment, may God bless you. Farewell.

CHAPTER XIV.

NOTES OF TRAVEL.

ORDERED TO NEW ORLEANS—EN ROUTE—NEW YORK—THE METHODIST BOOK CONCERN—REV. DR. PORTER—SANITARY FAIR—BROOKLYN—ON BOARD THE STEAMER UNITED STATES—OUT AT SEA—ARMY OFFICERS—THEIR WICKED CONDUCT—GAMBLING—PROFANITY—DISLOYALTY—SUBLIMITY OF THE OCEAN—MOOREHEAD CITY—BEAUFORT, N. C.—COLORED SCHOOLS—MISS LUCKEY—SEA SHELLS—OFF AGAIN—PREACHING AND FISHING ON SABBATH—OPINION OF AN OLD TAR—KEY WEST—PORPOISES AND FLYING-FISH—GULF OF MEXICO—OFF THE MISSISSIPPI—PILOT TOWN—THE SEA GULLS—UP THE RIVER—FORTS JACKSON AND ST. PHILIP—QUARANTINE HOSPITAL—THE COLORED PEOPLE—"GLORY TO GOD"—ARRIVAL AT NEW ORLEANS—DESCRIPTION OF THE MISSISSIPPI RIVER—ALGIERS.

MY appointment as Hospital Chaplain, by President Lincoln, and its confirmation by the Senate, with the order to report for duty in the Department of the Gulf, at New Orleans, has already been referred to. In obedience to orders, I prepared to embark for my destination, and reached New York on the afternoon of Friday, April 14th, 1864. Having never been in this magnificent city before, I determined to improve the time by looking around me and visiting a few places of interest. I may here state that I was somewhat disappointed in my expectations of the great metropolis. The apparent disorder prevailing in every department of business, the rush and hurry of men, the arrangement of the streets, and the generally confused aspect of things, presented a striking contrast to the staid and regular character of the city of Brotherly Love, with which I was familiar. A stranger in this modern Babel cannot repress a feeling of commiseration for his fellow-beings who are doomed to live, labor, and pass their daily existence in such a place.

As a Methodist preacher, the first object of interest I felt inclined to acquaint myself with, was the great Book Concern, at 200 Mulberry St., the central source of our denominational literature, and the head-quarters of our great missionary and other evangelical institutions.

Accordingly, I took a survey of this renowned locality, externally, and in its interior arrangements.

The impression made upon my mind was, that in regard to accommodations, we are far behind the times. I am glad to know that others more recently suggest, and insist upon a change of location, to Broadway, for instance, where buildings of suitable respectability and magnitude may be erected and occupied by our agents and editors.

The spirit of the times, the credit and character of Methodism, and the actual necessities of the business demand such a change.

I had the honor of meeting Rev. James Porter, D. D., one of our worthy book agents, during my walks about the "Concern." The doctor is said to be one of the shrewdest of that clear-headed, active, and enterprising race denominated "Yankee," and here, it would seem, he is in his native element, with scope as wide as the hemisphere for his planning faculties, and a routine of urgent daily duties and responsibilities to meet, that would set some men crazy. Dr. Porter, however, maintains his equilibrium, good humor, and systematic activity in his intercourse with visitors, and correspondence with the thousands whose tastes and wishes are to be consulted in the prosecution of the complicated business devolving on our agents.

To say that I was delighted with Dr. Porter, and that I have the utmost confidence in the capacity, integrity, and management of both Carlton and Porter, our agents, at present, is saying but little. May they be long spared to the church; for if ever the right men were in the right place, I believe the General Conference has hit the mark in their continued appointment.

The agents, and the editor of the Advocate, our great thunderer, stand very closely related to the whole family of Methodists, and I regarded it as no ordinary privilege, after many years of business connection with them, during which I frequently felt like doing as the Indian said, "shake hands with them in my heart," to meet them face to face, amid the machinery, which keeps the wheels in motion, and our system vigorous in its contemplated plan to conquer the world.

I next visited the great sanitary fair for the benefit of our brave soldiers and their families, and was led to thank God for having put it into the hearts of the good people of New York to devise so liberally for this worthy object. Many a sick and wounded soldier has sent his prayers and blessing to Heaven for the unknown benefactors who have lavished their means to contribute to his welfare.

On Sabbath morning, the 17th of April, I attended Divine service at the Seventeenth Street M. E. Church, a spacious and beautiful edifice, filled with a large and attentive congregation. I was privileged to hear the Rev. Dr. Crooks preach two very able sermons morning and evening.

Next day, April 18th, I crossed the East River to the city of Brooklyn, and was much pleased with its appearance, from the short stay I was permitted to make.

The steamer United States, on board of which I had secured a berth, was all ready to sail on the 19th, and bidding farewell to terra firma for a while, I went on board, and soon the harbor was left behind, as we rapidly neared the narrows, and then stood out to sea. I found the officers of the boat kind and gentlemanly. Quite a large list of army officers were passengers, the majority of whom soon displayed their ruling passion, and kept up their favorite pastime of gambling, swearing, and drinking during the entire voyage.

I have known some of these miscalled gentlemen, so infatuated by the vice of gambling, as to continue without intermission all night. I was pained by the reflection that so many men entrusted with important and respectable positions should be so immoral, profane, and recklessly wicked, in the face of the prevailing Christian sentiment of the country, and while so many associations in the north are engaged to Christianize and save the men of our noble armies. What society, I thought, will undertake the task of teaching our officers to respect themselves and fear God, to read the Bible and keep the Sabbath day holy; to countenance morality, prayer, and religious profession among the private soldiers, a thing many of them now prevent out of sheer wickedness?

And yet, it is a fact, that these corrupt and dissolute fops, who by the partiality of friends and the power of influence have obtained their shoulder straps, must admit that the bravest and best men of their commands are the men who pray and try to live a Christian life.

The reason why many of our army Chaplains have not succeeded better, is because of the needless, and wanton opposition, which some of the officers have shown to their work. Numbers of these seem to be more opposed to the principles of religion than they are to the principles of the rebellion, and show more determined obstinacy in contending against the cause of God, than they have ever manifested on the field of battle, against the rebels.

During this voyage I was led to pray, "O God have mercy on all officers of our army who speak of religion with contempt; who sneer at Chaplains and their work; who would drive from the ranks every praying man; and would, if they could, in their shallow-brained nonsense, and corrupt-hearted purposes, reason Thee out of existence, and the Bible into the fire! Pity, Lord, all such ninnies, and for Christ's sake make their hearts as soft as their heads, Amen."

Another feature of character was developed during my observations among these men, which I am ashamed to be compelled to notice and make public. Here we had fellows commissioned by the government and sworn to loyalty, who evinced the spirit of downright treason, and talked flippantly about those in authority, as if they were engaged to support the cause of Jeff. Davis and the Devil, and bring discredit to the country, for whose service and defence they had been engaged. When the time comes to hang traitors, I hope the Secretary of War will string up a few who have, from Major-General down to Second Lieutenant, showed the strongest sympathy with rebellion, and absolute hatred to liberty and Union.

After this tedious disgression, let us return to the voyage. April 20th, out of sight of land. Above, the sky; around, a boundless waste of water.

This was my first experience on the mighty ocean, and the sensations awakened in my mind were peculiarly grand and awful. The prominent idea that took possession of me was the immensity, grandeur, and almightiness of God. Truly He "rides upon the stormy sky, and calms the roaring seas." Standing on deck, and watching the giddy waves roll and dash against the bulwarks of our noble ship, the language of the poet occurred to me as the sublime and fitting expression of my feelings:

"Great source of being, beauty, light, and love!
Creator, Lord! The waters worship thee.
Ere thy creative smile had sown the flowers,
Ere the glad hills leaped; or the earth
With swelling bosom waited for her child;
Before eternal love had lit the sun;
Or time had traced his dial-plate in stars;
The joyful anthem of the ocean flowed,
And chaos like a frightened felon fled,—
While on the deep, thy Holy Spirit moved."

April 21st, the sea calm, and our vessel speeding on her southward course. To-day an incident occurred which might have resulted in terrible disaster, but for timely remedy. The ship caught fire, and for a moment confusion and consternation reigned. The fire, however, thanks to a kind Providence, was speedily extinguished.

Arrived at Moorehead City, N. C. this evening. This is a small village situated on a very barren tract of land, with no object of interest to attract the attention of the curious, or please the tourist who is seeking the picturesque and beautiful in sea-shore scenery. The government has a general hospital at this point, which appeared to be conducted and kept in good condition. Rev. W. C. Whitcomb is the Chaplain. He is an intelligent and deeply pious Minister of Christ. One of the soldiers on board our vessel, who had been sick, was removed to the hospital and died there very suddenly. I attended his funeral while we remained.

The government has erected a strong fort near this place which commands the channel and guards the entrance to both Moorehead City and Beaufort, another poor straggling village on the opposite bank of the river, about one mile and a-half farther up. It presents a better appearence from a distance than the reality on closer inspection will be found to exhibit. There are two colored schools there; one appears to be in a flourishing condition, under the management of a Miss Luckey, of New York. The coast is covered with beautiful sea shells, but we had no time to get up a collection for future use, to adorn the parlor of our prospective home. The Sabbath came while we were in port, and I took occasion to preach a sermon as well as to get up a patriotic meeting on board our ship.

April 28th, received four hundred and fifty colored troops on board, and found them to be orderly and soldier-like in all their deportment. Left port and turned our course direct for New Orleans on the 29th. During the 30th we were steaming away down the South Carolina coast, with nothing remarkable to disturb the monotony of our voyage.

May 1st being Sabbath, I preached on board. The sailors have been fishing all day, and succeeded in catching a number of king fish, weighing from sixteen to twenty-five pounds each.

One of the old Jack tars declared to me that fish in the sea always bite better on Sabbath, than on any other day of the week.

May 2d, off the Florida reefs, in the Gulf Stream, where the water forms a rapid current always setting one way. The porpoises swim along-side of our ship in droves, and great quantities of flying-fish are seen on the surface.

May 3d, in the Gulf of Mexico, and going at the rate of ten knots an hour, sea very rough, and Key West to be seen in the dim distance.

We reached the mouth of the Mississippi River on the 5th of May. Found quite a number of boats there. A small village located near the outer bar is called Pilot Town. We were cordially welcomed by the sea-gulls, who seemed glad to see us, and were boisterous in their overtures of friendship as they followed us up the river in large flocks. There is a bar formed across the mouth of the river by deposits constantly coming down with the current. This impediment frequently detains steamers of heavy draught sometimes for days before they can proceed up the river.

Fort Jackson is located on the right bank of the Mississippi, and Fort St. Philip on the left, at a distance of thirty-six miles from the mouth, and seventy-eight miles below the city of New Orleans. They were both objects of great interest to us as we steamed past, and scanned them closely. They appear very strong, and well arranged to resist attack; but the brave old Admiral Farragut and his thundering mortars, with Major General Butler's forces, made quick and effectual work when they combined to reduce them and the traitorous crew who resisted the legitimate authority of the government. The quarantine hospital is on the left bank, seventy-two miles below the city. All steamers and vessels are here overhauled by a surgeon appointed for that purpose, and if any on board are found sick with contagious or dangerous diseases, the vessel is detained ten days or more.

During our passage up the river, many of the colored people appeared along the shore cheering and bidding us welcome; some of them were shouting, "Glory to God." Even the little children appeared to be filled with a frenzy of joy, and would frequently exclaim, "We are all free!" The appearance of these things to me was quite affecting, and will never be forgotten by those who witnessed such exhibitions of delight and gratitude.

On the 5th of May, 1864, at 9 P. M., we arrived at the city of New Orleans; and before closing this chapter, if the reader please, I will add a few words descriptive of the great Mississippi River, which I consider in many respects the most wonderful in the known world. This magnificent river is, on the average, from three-quarters to a mile in width, and from fifty to two hundred and fifty feet in depth. The channel is so bold that vessels of the largest class can lay up to its banks anywhere, and receive or discharge their cargoes without the aid of a wharf. The force of the resistless and never-ceasing flow of its waters is such that it is slowly wearing away its banks, and in some instances altering its own course. In front of New Orleans the river is over two hundred feet deep, and by the movement of the stream round a graceful curve, the opposite bank, upon which the town of Algiers, containing a population of over two thousand inhabitants, is situated, is gradually caving in; and in the opinion of many, the whole site of this town will in the course of time be washed away, and every vestige of Algiers be obliterated.

OBSERVATIONS IN NEW ORLEANS.

CHAPTER XV.

NEW ORLEANS.

OBSERVATIONS IN NEW ORLEANS—LOCATION—COMMERCIAL STATISTICS —DANGER FROM INUNDATIONS—EFFECTS OF A HEAVY SHOWER—DAMAGE TO CRINOLINE—SURROUNDINGS—LAKE PONTCHARTRAIN—STREETS AND PAVEMENTS—CLEANLINESS—HEALTH OF THE CITY—STREET CARS—BUILDINGS—TILES—GARDENS—SHRUBBERY—FRUIT TREES—THE REBELS, FALSE PROPHETS—STAGNATION IN IMPROVEMENTS—GENERAL BUTLER—HIS CLAIMS TO GRATITUDE—CHARACTER OF THE PEOPLE—A COSMOPOLITAN CITY—CHILDREN—"TYPES OF MANKIND"—INTELLIGENCE—NEWSPAPERS—VARIOUS LANGUAGES —A SECOND BABEL—RELIGION—GAIETY IN DRESS—FAST ARMY OFFICERS—A STRANGE FACT—AVOCATIONS AND HABITS—SUPPLY OF WATER—SLEEPING ACCOMMODATIONS—MOSQUITOES AND THEIR PROPENSITIES—PRIDE OF THE PEOPLE—FAST LIVING—AMUSEMENTS —HATRED OF NORTHERN PEOPLE—EPITHETS APPLIED TO THE UNIVERSAL YANKEE—THE DUTY OF THE NORTH—NEED OF EDUCATION—REBELS STILL—HOW BARBARISM MAY BE PREVENTED AND THE PEOPLE CONVERTED FROM TREASON TO LOYALTY.

HAVING become a resident for the time being of the Crescent City, so called because of its half moon formation around a sweep of the mighty river, on the west bank of which it stands, I propose to give some facts and features of its character, which to a stranger may prove of passing interest. The observations I have been enabled to make, by keeping my eyes and ears open, are noted at length, not for the purpose of contributing to history, but as a memorial of the period, which, in the performance of my duty, I passed within its limits.

The traveler from New York will have to pass over sixteen hundred and fifty miles, and from Washington eighteen hundred before reaching this point. The first impression made upon the mind of a stranger is one of wonder that such a large city should have been built where there seems to be constant danger of inundation. The surface of the ground is so low in places back from the levee, that but for this embankment, the river, the surface of which is higher than the ground, would sweep it away. Indeed it has sometimes occurred, that a break in the levee has threatened terrible disaster, and overflowed a considerable portion of the city.

A heavy fall of rain at times fills the place with water, and drives pedestrians off the streets; wooden bridges are swept away, and both men and horses, unaware of the traps before them, tumble into the culverts and channels left thus uncovered. Sometimes legs are broken, and other damages received, from attempting to navigate the streets in the low and level portions of the city. A gentleman or lady may go out dressed up in the neatest attire, and if caught in a sudden shower, have to wade homeward in the most pitiable plight, with their clean linen, or crinoline dismantled and bedraggled beyond all comparison. If there is an unusual quantity of rain, all travel must be suspended for a time, and boats become more convenient as a means of transit, than a hack or cab. This surplus of water, however, slowly disappears by a very good system of drainage, which only requires time, from the level nature of the land, to perform its important office.

I have sometimes been compelled to employ a vehicle to convey me from my boarding-house a few squares, otherwise I should have had to wade that distance, the water being from one to three feet deep.

New Orleans has a very interesting history, the facts of which, to be known, must appear surprising. Its first settlement was made by Bieunville, in the year 1718. At the time it passed from the possession of France to that of Spain in 1743, it contained a population of only a little over three thousand inhabitants. Eighty years then elapsed before it was ceded to the United States in 1803, at which time its population was only about eight thousand. But from the date of its cession to the United States, the city began to grow. Its dimensions became enlarged, and a rapid increase is noticed in its population. Now, after a little more than half a century from that time, we find it embracing a population of over one hundred and fifty thousand, covering an area six miles long and two wide, and adorned with such evidence of art and taste, as to equal almost any other city in the union.

This result, as may be seen, is owing to social and commercial intercourse with other cities in every part of our great republic.

This city not only made great progress in population, but situated as it is, near the outlet of the Mississippi, it received at its levees nearly all the products of the great and growing West. Its wealth, therefore, advanced proportionably, with its population and its commerce.

The first newspaper published in New Orleans was in 1794, and was called the "Moniteur." In 1860 there were published in this city, ten daily newspapers, besides several periodicals of a literary and commercial character.

Among the oldest of public buildings, is the "Charity Hospital," founded in 1786. Probably the oldest edifice of any note in the city, is a building erected for the use of the Ursuline nuns, about the year 1730, and known as the "Ursuline Convent."

It is very interesting to examine the increase of exports from about the date of cession to the United States in 1803. The exports then amounted to about three million and a half of dollars. In 1860, the exports amounted to *one hundred and eight million of dollars!* In 1841, the southern and western produce, received in the city, amounted to about eighty-two millions of dollars. In 1860, they amounted to one hundred and eighty-five millions!

The cotton crop received in New Orleans in 1836 was four hundred and ninety-five thousand and forty-three bales. In 1860, the number was increased to two millions two hundred and fifty-five thousand four hundred and fifty-eight bales. This was one half of all the crop raised in the entire cotton states.

Such, has been the wonderful increase of the city of New Orleans, in population and wealth, since the destinies of Louisiana were united with the other states of the great western republic.

And it will be observed, that in previous years, with all her advantages, she remained for half a century nearly stationary.

The banking system of this city, before the war, was regarded as the safest and best in the Union. There were eleven Banks, with an aggregate capital of about eighteen millions of dollars. Thus in every element of prosperity, it will be seen, that it was at its very highest and most flourishing condition, when the demon of secession invaded and entered the heart of the people.

The changes wrought during the past four years are fearful to note. From being the largest cotton market in the world, and counting her receipts by millions of bales, she now considers herself fortunate if she can receive a few thousand.

Her commerce has also fallen off fearfully. In 1860, two thousand two hundred and twenty-five clearances were issued from the custom house, covering a tonnage of one million two hundred and forty-eight thousand five hundred and twenty-six tons.

In fact, the city of New Orleans was the second in the United States, in the amount and value of her exports, and no city in the world counted at its wharves so large a number of steam-boats.

Yet, notwithstanding this great prosperity, the fanatical citizens seceded from the Union through whose influence and trade she had been brought out of her obscurity and insignificance, and had become influential and respected among the other great cities of this glorious country. But enterprise and capital are again finding their way in this direction, and investments are being made, which will have a tendency to revive the present prostrate condition of things. In my judgment, if the merchants are allowed to resume and pursue commerce in its legitimate channels, the speedy resuscitation of the business of the city cannot be a matter of doubt for one moment. Under the present regulations business is much more active than it was, and is rapidly increasing. That it will continue to increase and again in the providence of God under Yankee brain, energy, and industry, reach a position that shall challenge the wonder and admiration of the world, and even surpass her former greatness and glory, I have no hesitation to predict.

The overthrow of slavery, and the abominable aristocracy founded on this system, will enlarge and encourage general industry and popular enterprise.

LAKE PONTCHARTRAIN

gives to the city one of its chief attractions. This is a beautiful sheet of water located at a distance of six miles in a westerly direction from the city. The lake has been, and still is a great place of public resort, the steam cars making several trips a day to and from its shores. There are also two splendid shell roads extending from the city to the lake, which afford a beautiful means of travel; these roads being very smooth and level, they are used by large numbers of the citizens to drive out of an evening for health and pleasure, and occasionally to try the speed of their fast horses.

There are also two canals, or basins, extending from the river to the lake, through which a considerable amount of trade is carried on. It is surprising to a stranger to find large swamps, and dense tracts of woodland located so near the limits of a large city like this. If the swamps were cleared up and properly drained, and the woods cut down, the health and comfort of the inhabitants, in my judgment would be greatly improved. Fresh air is a great desideratum in this warm climate.

We look in vain for the beautiful suburban residences and country seats, which are found in the vicinity of all northern cities, in the neighborhood of New Orleans. Improvements are quite meagre, and there is but little to be seen on the outskirts that would attract the eye, or arrest the attention, except the immense fields of cotton and sugar cane, in all the richness and redundancy of their beautiful appearance. The orange-tree, the fig, lemon, banana, and pomegranate, abound everywhere around us, and present a very pleasant feature of the scenery. There is also a great variety of other species of fruit growing in and around the city.

The climate I found to be much more salubrious and

less changeable than I had anticipated; for instance, I was frequently told in the North by those who professed to know, that during the middle of the day, in the summer season, the heat would be almost suffocating, and in the evening an overcoat would be necessary for comfort. These conjectures and representations are quite incorrect. I may state here, that during the entire summer I spent here, I never needed an overcoat in the evening, but always found the temperature warm and pleasant. Of course it is warmer here than in the North, but those who imagine the heat to be so intense as to nearly burn them up alive, may be relieved by the assurance that there is a fresh and pleasant breeze which comes from the gulf, and greatly moderates the torrid heat of the summer season.

STREETS AND PAVEMENTS.

New Orleans can boast of having some of the most substantial flag-stone pavements, as well as some of the best paved streets to be found on this continent. They are, moreover, kept very clean, being swept and washed every twenty-four hours, so that filth and garbage is not allowed to accumulate anywhere. It is owing to this fact that the city is, unquestionably, at this time, the healthiest in the United States. Although this is the warmest (August, 1864), and considered the most unhealthy season of the year, yet the mortality report of the past week shows only one hundred and twenty-one deaths from all causes.

Several of the streets are very broad, with a beautiful lawn twenty-five feet in width in the centre. This lawn is covered with grass, with two rows of splendid shade trees, between which the track is laid for the street cars, with a well-paved carriage-way, about twenty feet wide on each side.

The street cars run regularly on all the principal thoroughfares every few minutes. The city railways differ from those in our Northern cities in some peculiarities. The cars are drawn by mules which usually proceed on a gallop. They have no conductors on some of the lines, the companies relying on the honesty of passengers, who are expected to deposit their exact fare in a box provided for that purpose. The driver is allowed to change your money, but in no case is he permitted to deposit it. This arrangement appears to me, to work well, as every person is under the eye of his fellow-passengers, and also that of the driver, until he forks over his picayune.

BUILDINGS.

There are quite a large number of fine granite buildings in the city, but of dwellings, the majority are frame structures, one or one and a-half stories in height. The old-fashioned Spanish style predominates largely in these buildings, and they are mostly covered with "tiles." The sight of them brought vividly to my recollection the bold and emphatic declaration of Martin Luther, the great reformer, which has aided to give immortality to his name. Many of the private residences of the city are set back from the street, with a large yard in front filled with charming flowers and refreshing shade trees. Some of these private residences occupy an entire square, and give a beautiful variety with their luxuriant gardens, and embowered surroundings, resembling West Philadelphia for splendour and taste.

IMPROVEMENTS.

It could hardly be supposed that improvements would progress anywhere during the period in which our country was engaged in a fierce struggle for national life. Here there is utter stagnation in this department, and the contrast is indeed remarkable when we look at the facts and figures relating to this subject in Philadelphia alone. In 1863, there were three thousand five hundred substantial brick buildings erected there, and this in the midst of war's alarms and the constant call for men to recruit the wasted ranks of our armies. The rebels of the South have proved themselves false prophets in everything, and in no particular more signally than in this: that business would be entirely suspended, and that grass would grow in the streets of our principal northern cities in consequence of the war. On themselves, by their wicked rebellion, these predictions have been turned with a vengeance, and it is true of many a town, all over the South, that grass actually is growing on their paved streets and places of former prosperity in business.

But while industry has been crippled, business broken

up, and agricultural improvements almost entirely suspended in this city and vicinity since the outbreaking of the slaveholders' rebellion, we discover some indications of a revival. One most important matter is receiving needed attention; that is, the drainage of the swamps, and other subjects, very intimately connected with the general health and prosperity of the people.

Whatever may be said or thought by these bitter foes of the North in regard to Major General Butler, his name will live and be encircled with renown to later generations, for the sanitary measures and general improvements he suggested and inaugurated here. He did more for New Orleans than any man living. Our present exemption from the usual epidemics of the season, is owing in a great measure to his system of drainage—street cleaning, and attention to the poor.

About forty-five thousand of the hungry and suffering were fed by him; the lazy and idle were compelled to bestir themselves, and cleanliness became the law of life under his reign. No man has been more bitterly maligned, North and South, than he; yet the day may come when a monument will be erected to his worth even here, and the country will remember his services with as much pride and vastly more gratitude than those of many who cut a higher figure and made more noise during their day of brief authority.

All Union men in New Orleans concur in saying General Butler was "the right man in the right place."

THE PEOPLE.

In general appearance the people of New Orleans differ from those of northern cities in many particular traits and shades of character. Here you may meet with all conceivable sizes, shapes, ages, complexions, and nationalities. The author of the "Types of Mankind" would find here a wide field of investigation, in pursuit of his favorite study, and abundant material for a few more volumes treating on the endless varieties of the *genus homo.*

The population seem to be partial to out-door life, as at all hours of the day and evening you may encounter crowds on every street. A more prolific place for children it would be hard to find. Thousands upon thousands of them swarm in the various thoroughfares, and are seen on door-steps, side-walks, and in every possible nook and corner. The blending of races and colors apparent, suggest curious, if not sad reflections, and the palpable fact that multitudes of them are illegitimate, and consequently poor, friendless, and homeless, excites indescribable pity, when we remember the hopeless poverty and abandonment to which they are heirs.

The cosmopolitan character of the city suggests a reason for this order of things. The bringing into such close proximity so many nationalities, has produced a greater individuality and intensity of character here than elsewhere. Good and bad qualities are developed in a more positive and earnest manner than would be likely where some preponderating influences might mould and control the mass.

It is supposed that one half the population of the city are foreigners. A large proportion of their descendants remain so, to all intents and purposes, and their ideas of religion and law are as marked and strange as though they had been born abroad.

It is true that a great many of the people are refined and intelligent. The habits and manners of this class are more nearly allied to the French standard than any other. More than one third of the whole population are either French, or of French descent, which accounts for that style and suavity among them peculiar to the people of France.

In their bearing toward strangers they are for a time distant and reserved, but invariably polite and kind. As acquaintance ripens they become more free and familiar, and are excessively courteous at all times to ladies.

THEIR LANGUAGES.

I have concluded that the people of this city speak more languages, jargons, and gibberish, than the celebrated Elihu Burritt could ever hope to master. Apparently there is as great a confusion of tongues as existed among the bricklayers at the tower of Babel! A continued hum of voices, from male and female, comes upon your ears, in which are mingled the low guttural sound of "mine fader land," the musical ring of the Spanish, the sharp intonations of the French, with the mellifluous roll of the Italian, and occasionally a word of honest, hearty Anglo-Saxon, or a "bit of the brogue," to remind you that you are not in Naples, but in New Orleans, an American city.

I would suppose that at least two thirds of the people speak French, and apparently nine tenths use some other than the English. The reason for this excess of foreign dialects in the street is, as I have been informed, that many of the citizens have an understanding among themselves not to speak English on the street, in order to prevent the Yankees from understanding their conversation when they wish to exchange views on the state of the country.

It is a strange fact, that quite a number of them cannot speak the English language. Another singular fact is, that several of the newspapers of the city are published one-half in English, and the other half in French. It requires some energy and self-denial in a northern man to bring himself to remain here long at a time, on account of the wide dissimilarity existing between his views and tastes, and those with whom he is brought in daily contact. I have sometimes heard northerners playfully remark, that they were sick of this interminable jargon, and wanted to return to America! The manners and customs of the majority of people here are not American. They seem to take a pride in maintaining the usages, and following the customs of Europe.

RELIGION.

The Roman Catholic religion has the ascendancy in wealth and numbers. The following is a correct list, so far as I have been able to ascertain, of the different Protestant Churches within the limits of the city. Seven Presbyterian; seven Methodist Episcopal; three German Methodist; three Baptist; four Episcopalian; and one Unitarian. These churches had quite a large membership before the war; but as many of the members, and ministers too, went into the rebel army, I cannot give a correct list of their numbers.

The Methodist Episcopal Churches at the time of this writing are all under the charge of the Rev. J. P. Newman, D. D., of New York, and the Doctor manages to have all the pulpits filled by loyal ministers of the gospel every Sabbath. The Young Men's Christian Association has lately been reorganized under the immediate control of the different Christian denominations, and promises to become an instrumentality of good in the community.

The people of the city are considered as a general thing to be fond of gaiety, and are great votaries of fashion. The ladies are up with the times in all the new improvements in Paris millinery and stylish dress. Articles of foreign production always receive the preference, and home manufactures are discarded as unsuited to their wants.

Among those who dress very gay at present, I must include a number of our army officers, particularly the staff officers, who may have little else to do than adorn their persons with all the gew-gaws and trappings, which are thought necessary to set off a gentleman. And it is a noticeable fact here, as well as at other places occupied by our soldiers, that the most fashionable and showy, those who drive the finest team, and "go it," with the most reckless disregard to expense, belong to the Quartermaster's Department!

The avocations of the people are as varied as their character and habits are diverse. In this respect also you are reminded of European and Asiatic cities. The shoemaker or cobbler takes his bench out into the open air, and plies his craft under the eye of the multitude. Here are eating booths; yonder, fruit stalls; and farther on, you come in contact with candy shops, pea-nut stands, cake wagons, and boot-blacking establishments.

The picayune is the smallest amount of money in use here, and you cannot purchase a row of pins or a needle without paying the five cents. The cent piece so common in all retail business in the north is seldom seen "on change" in this city.

The meals are usually taken—in the morning from seven to nine, dinner from two to five, P. M., and tea from seven to nine, in the evening.

Rain-water, when on hand, is generally used for drinking and cooking purposes. It is secured in large cisterns, which form a necessary appendage to every dwelling.

The nature of the soil precludes the possibility of obtaining good water from wells; and during a continued dry spell the supply in the cisterns becomes very offensive, unless improved by the addition of ice. Ice, however, is a luxury which because of its cost, the poor cannot afford to enjoy. It has been sold at ten cents a pound during the warm season.

The accommodations for sleeping are somewhat peculiar, and in my judgment very superior. The beds, and bedsteads, are the best I have ever seen. An admirable contrivance is attached to each, by which musquito bars are used, and afford the sleeper a sure defence against attack during the night-watches. If ever poor plagued humanity needed fortifications against these guerrillas, it is in New Orleans; for a more rampant, blood-thirsty, and persevering foe, never laid siege to a citadel, or fought harder for spoils than they do. I think they bite the severest, when they do get a chance, and are the biggest, wickedest, and most noisy fellows I ever encountered.

For nine months of the year they wage war, and by all the modern tactics of corps, division, brigade and battalion drill, by skirmishing and flank movements they environ you, and like the chivalry of their native south, seem determined to conquer their rights, or die in the last ditch.

Nothing can exceed the luxury of lying down inside your "bars" of a midsummer night, and feeling secure from their voracious bills, as they hum around your room, and try to "come it," but find an abatis in their way, which effectually checks their advance, and allows you to fall gently asleep amidst the music of their wrath.

The arrogance so notorious in southern society, puts on its loftiest airs in this city. It is amusing to witness these scions of an imaginary nobility strut about as if they were lords of creation, and look down with supercilious disdain on northern people as beneath their notice. It chafes them very much to be confronted by a common sense Yankee, who returns their contempt with interest, and a little mixture of pity in it, and takes occasion to remind them that their foolish "airs" are all bosh, that their glory has departed, and that the saddest day they ever saw, was the day they went into ecstacies over the firing on our time-honored flag, which they tried to dishonor and bring to the dust, but which now and ever shall float proudly over their heads, the symbol of authority and power to which they must bow in obedience, although in their hearts they continue to curse it, and the benign government it represents on land and sea.

Many of the people here live *fast*, that is, beyond their means, and are dissipated in their habits. Living, as a large number of them did heretofore, on the sweat and toil of the poor negro, and now disinclined to work or apply themselves to business, these drones of society must seek some other latitude, and leave the field to popular enterprise and honorable labor.

All places of public amusement are patronized very

liberally. Wherever cheap amusement is to be had, you may see a moving mass of human beings eager for it, pressing into the theatres and beer gardens, and following street organs and itinerant fiddlers, apparently carried away by the vapid and supernatural trifles which waste valuable time, and cost a great deal of money.

SPIRIT OF THE PEOPLE.

It is a fact that the great majority of men, and women, too, in this city, and I suppose in all parts of the South, still hate and despise Northern people. Generations have been succeeded by generations, who seem to have been born and reared up with this bitterness predominant in their nature. Although compelled to depend on the great enterprising North for many of the essentials of life, yet they take delight in sneering at everybody and everything of Yankee origin, as though they were the benefactors and owners of the whole domain. I have traveled through five different Southern States, and spent six years of my life in slave territory, and have been irresistibly led to the conclusion that a degree of estrangement and repugnance, and deep-seated hatred prevails on their part, which will require time and determined treatment to eradicate. For years before the war their insults were carried even to the National Congress, and vented everywhere, and in every possible form against us. During the war this spirit has assumed the shape of downright ferocity, as may be remembered at the first Bull Run Battle, at Lawrence, Kansas, and at Fort Pillow, at which places they murdered many of our citizens and soldiers in cold blood.

Their treatment of, and bearing toward our prisoners, also furnishes evidence that cries out against their humanity, honor, and religion, and must live a stinging and lasting reproach and lie to their boasted chivalry.

I do not believe they are changed one whit for the better, or that kindness and leniency will cure them or bring them to a better mind.

Their show of allegiance to the government, I believe, to be all a sham, and that they, or any considerable portion of them, are converted from treason to patriotism, is merely moonshine.

Although soundly thrashed, they have the unblushing assurance to keep alive their favorite epithets applied to all Northern people of "mudsills, loafers, petty jobbers, miscreants," and "the scum of creation!"

Men of the great north and west, show these deluded mortals that you are not their *inferiors*, as they imagine! Educate them to broader views, and make the whole south, by your brain and enterprise, what it ought to be, in common with the undivided Union, to which you have bound it as with hooks of steel, "the land of the free" and the home of civil and religious liberty! I am firmly persuaded that the so-called Confederacy, even had it gained independence and general recognition, would have been short-lived, poverty-stricken, and as effete and useless as are now many of the miserable States of South America, where intelligence is beclouded, liberty dead, the people priest-ridden, and where barbarism is coming slowly and surely back again.

As an integral part of the "Universal Yankee Nation," there is a dawning of hope for the cities and people of the late rebellious States. Let the light shine and spread until darkness and hate shall be buried forever, and this motto so dear to our God-directed nation be written everywhere, not only on our banners, but on all hearts: "Virtue, liberty, and independence."

CHAPTER XVI.

OBSERVATIONS CONTINUED.

THE CLAY MONUMENT—IMMORTAL WORDS—REBUKE TO TREASON—THE JACKSON STATUE—"THE UNION MUST AND SHALL BE PRESERVED"—PUBLIC SQUARES AND CIRCLES—CUSTOM HOUSE—CITY HALL—STATE CONVENTION—EMANCIPATION—ST. CHARLES HOTEL.

THE Clay Monument is located in the centre of Canal St., near St. Charles. This is an eligible position, and reminds one, by its surroundings, of the Merchants' Exchange in Philadelphia. The street cars start from this point every few minutes for different parts of the city. The hacks and cabs congregate here also for the convenience of the public.

This beautiful monument to the memory of the distinguished statesman who, for sage counsel and far-seeing philanthropy, stood peerless in his day among the renowned men of the nation, reflects the greatest credit on the body who projected and the artist who executed it.

The imposing statue represents Clay in a standing posture, as if delivering one of his masterly arguments or orations. The front overlooks the father of waters, which rolls on its irresistible tide to the ocean, and although mute in marble stillness, yet there seems a voice in it which utters a stern rebuke to treason and rebellion.

Major General Butler caused the following extract from one of his great speeches on the slavery question to be chiseled in legible characters on the front base of the pedestal:

"IF I COULD BE INSTRUMENTAL IN ERADICATING THIS DEEP STAIN, SLAVERY, FROM THE CHARACTER OF OUR COUNTRY, I WOULD NOT EXCHANGE THE PROUD SATISFACTION WHICH I SHOULD ENJOY, FOR THE HONOR OF ALL THE TRIUMPHS EVER DECREED TO THE MOST SUCCESSFUL CONQUEROR."

Noble words! which possess a significancy in these evil times, that never were attached to them before, and definitely assigns to their author a high place among the immortal band whose hearts beat strong and high for universal freedom.

The Jackson Monument forms the main attraction of the square which bears its name. It is located on the levee, in the French portion of the city. It is one of Mills' equestrian statues of the hero of New Orleans, and from its symmetry and beauty, challenges the admiration of all who behold it. General Butler, in his efforts to right up things in his department, quickly discovered something wanting, in the completeness of this monument also. The rebels, among their first acts of vandalism, had effaced certain letters which were engraven on it, and he forthwith had the obliterated record restored. It is the world-renowned declaration, "THE UNION MUST AND SHALL BE PRESERVED." Under this as their rallying cry the hosts of the north have marched forth to battle. In the spirit of these great living words, thousands have fought and nobly fallen, and with a firm faith in them, as the sheet anchor of our hopes for the future, and a birth-right of happiness to unborn millions, "the last man and the last dollar," have been pledged to suppress the rebellion, and preserve our glorious Union.

I could not repress a rising wish, while frequently gazing on the monument, and lingering over this declaration that the man who uttered it, or one with his spirit and determination were living to-day, who could comprehend the depth of iniquity involved in rebellion, and with all the resources placed at his command, push on the war until not a fragment or vestige of treason should be left in the land. O! for a second Andrew Jackson, with the nerve to punish this stupendous crime as it deserves, and deal with *half-way men*, and *milk and water policy*, in a manner that would compel obedience and unconditional submission to the national authority.

PUBLIC SQUARES.

New Orleans possesses several beautiful public squares, which as "breathing places," or as they are termed in London, "the lungs of the city," are of great value to health and recreation.

La Fayette Square is located in front of the City Hall, on St. Charles Street. It is tastefully laid out, and forms one of the most popular places of resort.

Jackson Square is the handsomest park in the city. Here the equestrian statue of the brave old hero already referred to stands, and the grounds are filled with choice flowers, shade trees, and shrubbery of every variety, and trimmed and tended with skill and care.

Congo Square is located on Rampart street, and derives its name from the district in Africa which bears that name. It is devoted to the use of the colored people, who hold their convocations and festivities there.

There are several other attractive squares in different parts of the city, and a place called "Tivoli Circle," which adds to its embellishment, and contributes greatly to the comfort and pleasure of the citizens.

THE CUSTOM-HOUSE is a noble specimen of architecture, and one of the most striking features of the city. It is built of granite, covers the area of an entire square, and, although it cost the government an enormous amount of money, is still in an unfinished condition. The post-office occupies a part of this building.

THE CITY HALL is finely located, fronting on La Fayette Square, and appears to have been erected at great cost. In this building the late convention held its sessions. Here they formed the new state constitution and passed the act of emancipation. It has been used as the seat of government since the state capitol at Baton Rouge was destroyed by fire.

THE ST. CHARLES HOTEL is famed throughout the country for its high reputation and first-class management. It is a grand, imposing, and commodious edifice, with heavy columns in front, which gives it a majestic appearance. It is conducted on the European plan, and is the finest building of its class in the city.

CHAPTER XVII.

OBSERVATIONS CONTINUED.

THE MORAL CONDITION OF THE CITY—INDIFFERENCE TO RELIGION—SABBATH DESECRATION—STREET CARS—COCK-FIGHTING—DRUNKENNESS—STATISTICS OF RUM TRAFFIC—SUNDAY THEATERS—MUSIC—REVELRY—THE CATHOLIC RELIGION—EFFECTS OF DISLOYALTY—FOREIGNERS AND THEIR VICES—GAMBLING-HOUSES—SLAVERY—THE DEVIL'S WORKSHOP—PRIDE AND POVERTY—A GREAT HOME MISSIONARY FIELD—A DIFFICULT WAY TO HEAVEN BY NEW ORLEANS.

I REMEMBER to have heard and read much, when a boy, of the wickedness of the people of New Orleans. No person, however, not actually conversant with the habits, manners, and character of the people here, can have a vivid realization of the magnitude and variety of the forms which vice, irreligion, and immorality assume in the crescent city. After being a resident here sufficiently long to know personally whereof I affirm, I must bear witness that the half has never been told me. The evidences which establish here a bad preëminence in regard to immorality abound on every side. After making due allowances for the unsettled condition incident to war, I may be allowed to state that I consider this one of the most immoral cities, according to population, in the whole Union.

There are thousands upon thousands who never attend

religious service anywhere, but give their whole time to the service of sin and the devil.

I have observed the following facts:

First. The claims of the Holy Sabbath are by many totally disregarded. No sacredness or sanctity seems to be connected with it.

Second. The theatres are open on the evenings of the Lord's day, and are generally crowded by men, women, and children, whose moral sense, if they ever had any, is by this means sinking into deeper degradation constantly. No sadder sight is conceivable, in the mind of a northern Sabbath observer, than to witness these great crowds of dying mortals, wending their way to the various haunts of amusement, and vice, when it would seem they ought to be engaged in prayer, and listening to the teachings of God's word.

Bands of music are out on balconies playing, and no means which may seduce and attract the multitude to Sabbath-breaking, is left untried. How often these sounds, so discordant amid the stillness of the holy Sabbath evening, have pained my heart, and made me wish and long to be beyond their influence.

Third. The street cars run all day on Sabbath, as on any other day of the week, and multitudes are seen riding in them, and in private carriages for mere pleasure.

Fourth. Cock-fighting is a popular pastime on the Sabbath, and attracts crowds to witness this barbarous practice, which is highly demoralizing in its influence.

Fifth. Drunkenness abounds. The hotels, grog-shops, saloons, and other places where whisky is sold, are crowded. There seems to be no restriction on the sale of intoxicating liquor, except the license, which is one hundred dollars, for every place of this character. There are six hundred and thirty-seven licensed groggeries, or, as they are here called "Coffee-houses," and many of them are temptingly open night and day.

There are five hundred and twenty-eight groceries, also licensed to deal in strychnine whisky, or what some one appropriately calls "damnation;" making in all eleven hundred and sixty-five places, where the public may purchase rum. This is a larger proportion than can be enumerated in any city of its population in Christendom.

It will also be noted, that in view of the heavy cost of license, they must all contrive to sell large quantities. to enable them to pay expenses. Thousands of barrels are therefore consumed annually; for they all seem to be making money, and amassing fortunes, by the manufacture of drunkards, and all the ills and woes which follow in the train, both here and hereafter.

Some apologize for this excessive use of intoxicating drink, on the ground that health demands a certain amount of stimulus. This I pronounce untrue. The men who take no intoxicating liquor enjoy the best health. Hear this, ye devotees of Bacchus, and all ye who encourage them in their ruinous course. It is a lamentable fact that some of our army officers have fallen into this delusion, and have become addicted to the same evil habits. It is perilous to themselves, and most prejudicial to others, by their influence and example. The surgeon that will advise you to this course, is likely to be a rum-sucker himself, and is therefore a blind guide, in matters of this kind. I have known patients to die in the hospitals crying "I am drunk," and why was this? Because the surgeon in attendance administered liquor.

What a fearful responsibility that Doctor will incur when he stands before the judgment-seat, who has used his authority to increase drunkenness, and under the derangement occasioned by intemperance, has sent souls into the presence of God their maker!

Sixth. The statistics of vice represent the city as cursed with houses of ill-fame, where unblushing licentiousness is going on day and night. Iniquity of this species is said to be utterly unbridled throughout the city.

Seventh. The few, comparatively, who attend church seldom go more than once on Sabbath, and are reasonably supposed to spend the balance of its sacred hours in idleness.

Eighth. Another cause, and perhaps the chief one, in accounting for the low state of public morals in this city, is, the prevalence of the Roman Catholic religion. The history of the past will show as the fruits of this system, a state of ignorance, and a standard of morality exceedingly low.

Ninth. The fact of disloyalty may be cited as a cause of immorality. Wherever the blight of secession and treason has appeared—there may be gathered the evidence of wrong-doing in every department of social life.

Rebellion was inaugurated against the light of conscience and convictions of right, and truth. Losing sight of their high and holy obligation to preserve allegiance to the "powers that be," general recklessness of character and conduct has here, as elsewhere been the result.

Tenth. The subject of education has not received the attention here which has been given to it in northern cities. Certain classes have been entirely neglected, and the tendency has been fatal to virtue and morality.

Eleventh. The foreign element in this city being, as I have shown, a large proportion of the population have brought their loose views and low vices with them from other lands, and in the enjoyment of a larger liberty than they ever had before give unrestricted development to their depraved habits, and help to demoralize community around them.

Twelfth. Gambling-houses abound and are constantly in full blast, decoying young men into their meshes, and destroying their morals.

This specific evil is regulated, or rather licensed by the authorities, and there is hardly a voice raised in condemnation of it. The press, which ought to be the conservator of good morals everywhere, is so submissive to public opinion, that it dares not speak out as it should on this question. A leading article in one of the papers recently said, "It is a very nice point, a delicate question;

and a great deal can be said on both sides; whether public morality can be best served by licensing gambling-houses, or enacting prohibitory laws against them."

Out upon such base subserviency, even in appearance, to the clamor of a depraved and perverted taste. The really moral and good people of New Orleans, as of all other cities, who look at the subject from a proper stand-point, must know that the prohibition of vice, not only prevents its commission very frequently, but is actually demanded as a safeguard for society.

Thirteenth. The existence of human slavery, after all, is the prime cause of that low state of morals for which this city is preëminent. This parent evil has brought forth an innumerable progeny of peculiar vices. It is the cause of idleness among the white population, and this is generally the source of bad habits. An idle mind, as the homely phrase has it, is the "devil's work-shop." While it would drive the poor bondman to his work by the lash, and chain him to his toil from day to day, it exempted the master and his race from earning their bread by the sweat of their own brow, as the great law of Scripture requires. The indolence engendered, therefore, by slavery, becomes a hot-bed for prolific sins.

I may add, to these facts, that there are numerous families who are too proud to attend church without paying their way, and yet, are so straitened in their circumstances, that they cannot afford to do it. They consequently remain away from worship, and parents, and children, are growing up without the influence of the means of grace.

Again, there are a very considerable number of young men, clerks, and artisans, who are here but temporary sojourners, their object being to make a fortune, and then, as they hope, to leave here for more congenial surroundings elsewhere. This class are entirely alienated from everything like religious influence, although many of them were brought up at their distant homes to respect the Bible and fear God.

With all these considerations before us, who can doubt that this city and vicinity, and, indeed, the state at large, is a very appropriate field for the work of home missions.

It is true, and I admit with great pleasure, the exception, that there are some excellent people here, as there are in other parts of the South. If there had not been a little salt this whole region would long since have been as Sodom. I assert, notwithstanding, that the picture here is substantially true of the great majority, and any comparison that may be instituted between the North and South, will show a large preponderance in the scale of morality in favor of the former.

I hope, and will earnestly pray for better days, when a free gospel shall here run and be glorified, and these tens of thousands who are without God and hope in the world, will be awakened powerfully, and soundly converted from the error of their ways.

At present, it is my deliberate judgment, that it is

no easy matter to go to heaven by the way of New Orleans.

I do not mean by this that a good man cannot maintain purity of life and conduct anywhere, but it is not at all desirable to be so circumstanced that the liability to fall into temptation is increased a hundred-fold. The possibility of falling from grace is one of the doctrines of my creed, and I have always believed that a Christian's safety and peace is best promoted by avoiding even the appearance of evil.

CHAPTER XVIII.

OBSERVATIONS CONTINUED.

FOLLY AND MADNESS OF REBELLION—AVERAGE OF RUNAWAY SLAVES —SLAVE HUNTING IN THE SWAMPS—"PIOUS" MASTERS—ENGLISH NEUTRALITY—MOTIVES OF THE BRITISH—A NUT FOR LORD JOHN RUSSELL TO CRACK—SECRET MEETINGS FOR TREASONABLE PURPOSES—CHARACTER OF THE POLICEMEN—INDIGNITIES TO UNION SOLDIERS—"STRAWS," SHOWING HOW THE WIND BLOWS—FOREIGN LANGUAGE A CLOAK TO TREASON—ROMAN CATHOLICISM FAVOURABLE TO DESPOTISM—DISLOYALTY OF THE WOMEN—HATRED OF THE FLAG—STARVATION UNDER JEFF. DAVIS' DYNASTY—PARTIALITY TO REBEL PRISONERS—THE TEXAN BATTLE-CRY—PETTICOAT GOVERNMENT—UNION OFFICERS IN THE HANDS OF DELILAH—HEART CAPTURES—FREE MASONRY IN THE SOUTH—NO AFFILIATION WITH YANKEES—UNACCOUNTABLE PARTIALITY OF THE POOR WHITES FOR THE SYSTEM OF SLAVERY—THEIR TRUE INTEREST AND POSITION—SABBATH-SCHOOL BOOKS AND RELIGIOUS PAPERS DESTROYED—MADNESS AND INFATUATION OF THE PRO-SLAVERY PARTY—THREE SECESSION MERCHANTS "DRIED UP"—"GLORIOUS NEWS!"—GOD ON THE SIDE OF THE UNION.

FROM the prosperity which had ever attended this state and city, since coming under the jurisdiction of the United States, and from the disposition which the people evinced to delight in the growing greatness of the "fair City of Perth," and in the advent of any, and everything that might add to her wealth, or enhance her beauty, it might reasonably be supposed they would have been the last to lift the hand of rebellion against our glorious government.

It is, however, a palpable fact, which history has put down on imperishable record, that against all experience, all obligation, and all her interests, she was as blind as the rest of her misguided sisters in their "wayward" course to dishonor and wreck. And imbibing the baleful spirit of treason, her leading citizens embarked their all in the false dogma of "State rights," or southern independence.

So pernicious were the teachings of these leading spirits, and so potent their influence, that it is the opinion of sensible and reliable men, nearly if not quite nine-tenths of the original citizens are either downright rebels, or in sympathy with their unholy cause. Jeff. Davis himself is no more disloyal than are many of these people to-day.

In their mad and baffled rage, they inform us that they hold the same relation to us of the north, that we did to England before the revolutionary war: that the causes which induced them to rebel, and the objects they have in view, are as pure, honorable and holy, as those of our fathers when they cast off the British yoke. What a delusion!

If they had reasons for resistance and rebellion against the parent government, why did they not present their grievances, as was done in former days to England, before firing on the flag? They may have had some imaginary and some real cause of complaint against northern men and some of the northern states; but they could find no fault with the general government, since it was at the very time of the outbreak, partly under the control of bold, bad men, thoroughly wedded to their own interests. Any charge of wrong, or oppression against it, would, if calmly and respectfully made, have been patiently considered, and if founded in truth, redressed. To allege that they were oppressed, or that their interests were disregarded, would have been false, and they know it. The enlightened sense of mankind testifies emphatically as to the *causelessness*, and the utter insanity of their course. Nothing could have occurred, more *suicidal* to New Orleans and her people than secession. Why then did they secede? Only twenty-eight of their slaves on an average, escaped annually to the north.

A larger number may have fled from the cruelty or lust of the master, or the lash of the soulless overseer, into the neighboring swamps; but would secession make the swamps less intricate or remove them further away? I have been informed that masters, professing to be *pious*, hunted their runaways in these places with bloodhounds, to recover possession of their human property!

The attitude of England toward us and toward the so-called Confederate States is one of strange inconsistency. It can only be accounted for by the cupidity and jealousy of that nation: first, to break down the colossal power of our growing and mighty Union; and secondly, to embrace every chance, whether the means be fair or foul, to make money. That the ambitious and selfish demagogues of the south were instigated and encouraged in the work of rending the Union in twain is not to be doubted; and that for once the biter has been severely bitten must be a source of high satisfaction to every just and honorable mind. It is the order of God in regard to nations as well as individuals, "With what measure ye mete, it shall be measured to you again." And the day may come when the doctrines of Lord John Russell and some of his hypocritical abettors may be convenient as a basis of action in certain coming contingencies. Let poor Ireland arise and strike for republican liberty, and then let us as a *neutral power* act toward England on the principles which English statesmen have laid down as law and right, the tables will be effectually turned, and if the old lion dares to growl, we can, by the help of God and the memory of Washington, turn to and whip the whole of them a *third time*. But it is to be hoped that no occasion of this kind will arise. Rather do we wish for universal peace, and cultivate "good will to men."

The future of this great nation is a fixed reality. England, southern aristocracy, and the devil combined, have not succeeded in impairing, one iota, our unity, perpetuity, and power. A brighter destiny than ever is before us. Our flag again floats over every foot of American soil. We stand shoulder to shoulder to defend that banner, to maintain the Monroe doctrine, to demand respect from European nationalities, and to take Mr.

John Bull by the horns at any time he becomes uproarious, and shake him down into propriety and repentance for his many and mean acts, of which he stands convicted at the bar of public opinion.

It is curious to observe the change that has come over the minds of the rebels in regard to their expected ally across the ocean. Deserting their sinking cause when his own schemes are hopeless, he has gained their hearty and undisguised contempt.

I have learned on good authority, that the rebels and their sympathizers in this city, hold secret meetings on certain evenings of each week, to devise ways and means to oppose and embarrass the government, and aid the cause of rebellion. It is also understood that they have agents engaged for pay, whose duty it is to frequent the hotels and other places where Union officers congregate, and collect all the information they can, and then make their report to the rebel head-quarters. I have myself seen these spies deliberately draw up their chairs near where our officers were engaged in conversation, and without seeming to be interested, attentively note every syllable uttered. I have found it to be a difficult matter at times to restrain my hands from their coat collar, and my feet from performing an act which, although undignified, is yet justly due to all such rascals. Kind and courteous treatment is lost on such bitter opponents of everything and everybody pertaining to the Union. They have upon all occasions treated us as enemies, while we have too frequently treated and trusted them as friends.

The police force of this city are considered by many to be of similar stripe with the majority of the citizens, that is—disloyal. There may be a few, and I believe *only* a few exceptions. As a body, I have seen enough to substantiate the charge I make against them. They show every symptom of gratification when they can arrest and misuse a poor straggling Union soldier that unfortunately falls into their hands; and this inhumanity always delights the rabble, whose contempt poured on our soldiers is a notorious and oft repeated fact. Indeed the police, the rowdies, and the most noted rebel citizens, are always on the best of terms, and I have no doubt, conspire together for their own nefarious ends. Many of them, it is known, have been in the rebel army, and after sundry campaigns, have now become *peace* officers in our midst. That such a thing as this can exist, is a disgrace—a burning shame; giving them the power to control to any extent the soldiers, who are here in the service of the government, defending its honor, and upholding its authority.

That part of the population who are foreigners by birth, and who have been educated to despise a republican form of government, very naturally fall into the position of hostile foes. They do not understand the nature and workings of our system, and are ever ready and ripe for revolution. We can make some allowances for this class, and only demand that they shall learn to adapt themselves to our usages, and respect our legitimate authority, or return to the old world, and allow their places here to be filled with better men. The insolence and ignorance of many of them is a great annoyance to those who love to breathe the pure air of freedom, and who love their land as they love their life.

It would seem to us that foreigners of all others ought to appreciate their position, and become the most intensely loyal to a country that has lifted them up out of degradation, and spread its wings of protection and plenty around them, to a degree they never could have reached under the despotic governments of Europe.

The absurd idea of erecting a kind of monarchy here in the South, for the purpose of maintaining the effete aristocracy which built its foundation on human slavery, took very generally with these foreigners; but the dream of their dynasty has melted away, and there will shortly be no room here for the friends of despotism. By right of conquest, the hardy, earnest sons of liberty, have made, and will maintain this undivided domain—"the land of the free and the home of the brave."

I have already adverted to the significant fact, that citizens here converse, when in the presence of Union men, in a language which they do not understand, and thus may indulge to the greatest extent in treasonable talk with impunity. Much of the jargon we hear in our intercourse with the more influential people, would, doubtless, if translated and understood, commit them to imprisonment and the penalty due to traitors.

The prominence of the Roman Catholic Church, and the blind adherence to her teachings which is given by multitudes, may account for their disloyalty. It is a well-known fact that this semi-political hierarchy is opposed to republican liberty. Of course there are individual exceptions by some devotees of this faith, who rise far enough above the spirit and teachings of "mother church," to appreciate the birth-right of freedom; but it is a matter of history that the large body of Romanists in these United States, have always voted according to the dictum of their priests, and the policy of the priests has ever been to seek and secure political power. Therefore, whatever party has promised them the largest advantage, has invariably secured their support.

We would not be uncharitable, or allow bigotry to pervert judgment, and yet we say that this body is loyal only so far, and in such proportions as her interests are subserved. It is to her great discredit, and must remain a stigma on her name, that during this terrible war, her bishops, priests, and people, have either taken sides openly with our enemies, or refused to say a good word in behalf of the Union cause. In fact, they occupy the position of the man on the fence in all such important issues, and are waiting to jump to either side as worldly policy may suggest.

I am glad to record such honorable exceptions as Bishop Purcell of Cincinnati, and some of the generals and officers of our army, whose hearts beat true for "Liberty and Union, one and indivisible." Such illustrious names as Rosecrans, Corcoran, Meagher, and the renowned Phil Sheridan, are noble types of loyalty and bravery, but this is not because, but in spite of the poor pitiful policy of a creed that bends before every blast, and overlooking settled principles adjusts itself to circumstances.

No press in the country has taught treason with a more virulent and persistent intent, than that under Catholic control. Between their papers published in New York or Boston, and the organs of the bogus Confederacy at Richmond, there has been a marked similarity of tone, and a perfect agreement in principle, so that ages cannot wipe out the record of complicity which this church has earned with the traitors of the South. The rebels seem to understand this matter, and boastingly claim the prestige and patronage of Roman Catholicism on their side, both in this country and abroad. It is said that the only foreign power that was fool enough to recognize the South, was that vested in an old man at Rome by the name of *Pio Nono!*

No doubt our Catholic population look with especial favor and approbation on the course of Napoleon with reference to Mexico, and that, true to all the past history of this Church, any change in human government would be desirable that secures to her the prospect of temporal as well as spiritual power.

It is confessed to be a darling and fundamental article

of her faith, that the Pope ought to be supreme head of the State—of all State governments—as well as sole arbiter of all moral, spiritual, and eternal interests relating to mankind: but the world has outlived such theories as this, and the nineteenth and twentieth centuries are not likely to retrace the progress of freedom's car, or relinquish the boon of liberty of conscience, to gratify the lust for power and ascendency which forms the leading characteristic of this Church.

From the stand-point here raised, we may be able to account for the indifference she has manifested for the success of the cause of human freedom, and the aid and comfort she has given to our enemies, not caring apparently which party, the insurgents or the loyal force, might succeed if this success should or could tend to her advancement.

On the 4th July, 1864, the Roman Church of this city, by her chief ecclesiastics, celebrated a "High Mass" for peace. What kind of peace, I wonder, would suit such pious rebels? Some compromise, doubtless, with ultra southern views, or concession to Jeff., Tom Walker, Napoleon, or the Pope, not forgetting a personage at the bottom of all their schemes, and familiarly known as "his Satanic Majesty." I had more faith in the music of fife and drum, and the arguments of one-hundred pounders, at that date, in securing peace, than in high-falutin display of mummery around the altars of a Catholic church.

It is exceedingly unpleasant to be compelled to class

the great majority of the women of this city with the most bitterly disloyal and unfriendly to the government represented by the Stars and Stripes.

They have various ways in which their hostile spirit is manifested, in the public streets, as well as at their homes. In dress it is easy to discern, by certain blending of colors, who are and who are not "sound on the eagle." An arrangement of red, white, and red ribbons or flowers indicates in a moment that the person is a reb. You will see this class avoiding all contact with others who sail under the good old red, white, and blue, and shunning, as if it were contagious, the presence of a Union officer or soldier. Their expressions, also, in the cars, and in other public places, are often intended to convey a stinging insult to persons of Union sentiments. Not one of them was to be found visiting the hospitals where our sick and wounded soldiers lay, while crowds of them sought admission among the rebel prisoners to load them with luxuries, and encourage them not to take the oath of allegiance.

It is strange that such a large proportion of the fair sex, should be on the wrong side, since it is a maxim that women almost by intuition are on the side of humanity, purity, and truth.

We have heard some of their children declare in company, to the great mortification of the haughty mother, that before the Federal fleet arrived off the city, they were reduced to corn bread and water as their daily diet; and notwithstanding many of these persons have been fed and clothed, their children saved from nakedness and starvation, and employment given to their husbands by the government, during the past two years, yet these very women are engaged night and day, in doing all they can to aid the rebellion.

Their disloyalty, and ingratitude, must be the result of that perversity and wickedness, which as we have seen, is everywhere cropping out as the fruits of the mania of secession.

I heard one of the ladies (?) of this city, urge a paroled Texan prisoner to gratify her by giving the Texan battle yell, and offering to reward him for so doing; but the poor Texan either had better sense, or was afraid to give the desired exhibition, and the other had to pass on without the coveted pleasure.

Our flag was a great eye-sore to these women. In one of the churches it was hung over the pulpit, and they requested that it might be removed, as the sight of it made them feel like fainting! Had it been the "stars and bars," the effect would have been different.

Many of these high-toned females know that the suppression of the rebellion will sweep away the chief prop on which it rests, that is slavery, and such a consummation is to them a deplorable calamity; for the force of circumstances will compel them to do what they have been educated to consider a disgrace, viz. *to work.*

If it should happen that some of them will have to take the oversight of their own kitchen, which now is left to the exclusive superintendence of "Dinah," they will feel like a cat in a strange garret, and will have to begin life anew, by devoting themselves to something more practical than novel reading and fine dress. Work will be to them the greatest of blessings, if they only knew it. The changes that are inevitable in the whole structure of southern society will conduce to better health and more happiness than has ever been the case before.

After all the abuse and scorn heaped upon General Butler, for his common sense views, and strictly just dealing with this people, it appears to any impartial mind that he was right in every measure tending to subjugate the obstinate and unmannerly bearing of these she rebels, toward a people who came as their best friends, and brought deliverance to their city, and security to their homes.

One remarkable fact in regard to these ladies, has arrested my attention: although they exhibit such contempt for the Yankees, yet strange to say, many of them have allowed their hearts to be captured and have gracefully yielded themselves up to the officers and soldiers of our glorious army.

With all their secession proclivities, I have not heard of one of them refusing to marry a good-looking Union officer, when the chance was fairly offered. A great many captures of this tender kind are reported, and so far as they go, will, I suppose, have some influence in restoring the Union.

Another matter forces itself on my pen. It may be contraband to say what I am about to write, but I take the responsibility. Some of the most designing and dangerous of these secesh women appear to have gained a wonderful influence over certain of our army officers, and can obtain any information, or secure any favor that suits their purposes. It is even whispered that they have wormed out secrets which have been rapidly transmitted to our enemies in the field, and which have turned against us the fate of more than one severe engagement. Now if such things are so, and there is strong probability of the charge being true, the officer who allows himself, and the cause he is commissioned and sworn to defend, to come under this kind of petticoat government, ought to be cashiered the service at once.

The rupture caused by secession extended not merely to political and civil relations, but also to every social tie and fraternal order in the south. It was sometimes intimated, when the cloud of war was gathering in blackness and fury in the horizon, and the wisest and best men of the nation were seeking some basis of compromise, that the ancient and powerful order of "Free Masonry" formed in itself a bond of union between north and south that no power could break or destroy. But the madness which seized the "chivalry," so perverted all their principles of honor and obligations of fellowship that they repudiated their brethren, and declared against affiliation with either lodges or members of the order beyond their own circumscribed boundary.

In New Orleans there are a number of lodges, and

the customary card of invitation to strangers was before the eye of the public, when a couple of our officers belonging to a regiment stationed here, concluded to seek admission, being members in high standing, and eligible to enter the portals of any lodge room in the world. They were *refused* admission, solely, as may be conjectured, on the ground of their uniform; when if they had been dressed in rebel gray, and belonged to the army of Jeff. Davis, no doubt they would have met with a warm welcome.

All who look at a transaction of this kind from the proper stand-point must see that such unmasonic conduct by the free masons of this city is a significant straw, which shows which way the wind blows. Non-intercourse is their policy as far as they can, and as long as possible, with those who have taken any part in vindicating the honor of their nation's flag.

If any human obligation can be stronger or more sacred than that just referred to, it is the common impulse and holy bond of the religion of Christ; but this has been trampled upon as recklessly as the other. Frequently they leave the house of God, because the minister officiating followed in prayer the requirements of the Divine word, and remembered at the throne of grace "all in authority." At other times they evince their contempt, if a pious soldier is called on to lead in prayer, or rises to relate his Christian experience.

I have known parents to encourage their children to destroy our Sabbath School library-books and papers, because they were supposed to contain something on the subject of slavery, or against that institution. They have also destroyed religious tracts, books, and papers, because they had a picture of our starry banner printed on the cover.

It struck me as a very remarkable fact, that many of the poorer people, who never owned a slave, were among the most rabid pro-slavery secessionists. They are so ignorant and deluded, it has not entered their mind that slavery has *kept them poor* and in a degraded condition; that by this system they have been placed at a serious disadvantage in all the relations of life; and that the rich owner of men and women looks down upon them as only a little removed from the negro in point of social condition, and to be used as the colored slaves are, for the exclusive benefit of the wealthy.

And yet these poor whites, of their own free will and accord, defend slavery, thereby increasing the causes which have made and which keep them dependent.

Let slavery be swept away, and their greatest disability—their worst enemy is removed. Then a chance will be opened to them for improvement and social elevation, which will result in self-respect, enterprise, and a larger equality.

Another "straw" which indicates the tendency of the times here, is the prominence and popularity given to such papers as the "New York News," "The World," and other northern sheets that have earned a "bad pre-eminence" by their opposition to the general government.

These papers have done us more harm, by misrepresentations of the state of affairs at home and abroad, and have given more aid and comfort to the enemy than can be estimated.

Even the officers and privates of our army are often led astray by their wholesale lies and secret inuendoes, and sometimes have wavered for a time in their faith, as it regards final success and the triumph of the principles of right over foul and cruel wrong, by such teaching.

I think the editors of such papers, with their fellow-traitors at Richmond and elsewhere, have richly earned the nation's reprobation, and when mercy asserts her sway, they ought to be among the exceptions, and either patronize a piece of hemp, or go to some penitentiary for the balance of their natural lives.

In case of a slight reverse to our arms at any point on the wide theatre of war, these disloyal people are the first to smell it out and magnify our losses, while their countenances express the highest exultation over their own success.

It is a hard discipline for loyal men who live in the midst of traitors to remain quiet and hopeful while their enemies sneer at them and rejoice over temporary advantages gained in their unholy cause. At such moments, what aggravates the case, is an increasing insolence, and more bold defiance in their bearing toward our army officers and the boys in blue.

Under such circumstances, it is really terrible to contemplate their infatuation. What are they seeking? To what lengths are they determined to proceed? Despotism, desperation, death, rather than defeat and the blessings of a free government! Bondage entailed on millions, and a tremendous per centage of the class doomed to hopeless slavery, their own offspring! A corner-stone for their fabric of nationality, of groans, tears, and unutterable, indescribable woe! This is secession.

If the news of our reverses lit up the countenances of secessionists in New Orleans, tidings of victory to the Union army was always a bitter pill. One day a news-boy was hurrying along with his extras, crying out the thrilling news of the capture of Atlanta; while passing three merchants, they ordered him to "dry up," and just at the instant, Lieutenant Eddy, son of Ex-Governor Eddy, of Rhode Island happened to be within hearing. He immediately exclaimed "Shoot those three rebels!" when all three in an instant retreated out of range, and took good care to "dry up" themselves, and keep in the back-ground for a time.

They tried to disbelieve, as successive dispatches came in, recounting our successes and the evident caving in of the rebellion, and to the very last persisted in hoping their dark cause would prevail. It must have been that they were given over to a reprobate mind to believe a lie and to reap what they had sown; for no intelligent mind with the Bible and its revealed God before him could see wherein, or how, consistently with the character of that great Being, and in a manner harmonizing with his attributes of justice and righteousness, a cause founded on such iniquity could flourish or succeed. He has declared "The day of vengeance is in mine heart, and the year of my redeemed is come." Let the slaveholder, therefore tremble; for retribution is before him; and let the oppressed rejoice: for with a strong hand, and a mighty arm hath the Lord set them free.

CHAPTER XIX.

OBSERVATIONS CONTINUED.

UNION MEN IN NEW ORLEANS—STATE CONVENTION—LEGISLATURE—HOW I RECEIVED NINETY DOLLARS FOR ONE PRAYER—LOYAL LADIES—DELIVERANCE FROM REBEL MISRULE—A MINISTER BIDS HIS SLAVES GO FREE!—A BRIGHTER DAY AT HAND.

IT affords me the greatest pleasure to turn over a new leaf in my narrative, and make memorial of the fact that pure patriotism has existed, and still lives in this city, in the midst of an overwhelming tendency to disloyalty. A few ladies and gentlemen from the beginning of the war, and through all its varying fortunes, have been found true to the Union.

The arrival of the Federal fleet and armies, was, to this class of persons a "great salvation," and the presence of those who "rally round the flag" in their beloved city, is to them a matter of sincerest joy. Like an oasis in the desert is the smile of their face and friendly grasp, where scowling treason, and bitter hatred meets the northern man.

Among the number who composed the State Convention which passed the emancipation act, we find these prominent and fearless champions of the right; and in the Legislature, now in session, such honored names as R. K. Howell, Judge Durell, T. J. Durant, and men of their stripe, are standing up boldly and bravely, to remodel the whole structure of society, and carry out the provisions of the new Constitution, in its requirements bearing on human liberty and a just recognition of the rights of all.

The Legislature of Louisiana appropriated one thousand dollars to pay the ministers for opening the sessions with prayer, and I received ninety dollars as my portion. I might add that I was never paid before or since so well for offering one prayer.

The triumph of the government, and the utter subjugation and overthrow of the rebellion, will be to the Union people of New Orleans the dawn of a glorious era. They have been taunted, mocked, imprisoned, and persecuted without mercy. Some have lost property, and not a few have sacrificed their all in allegiance to their country, during the dark days of rebel misrule. What a victory it will be to them when the accursed Confederacy and all its allies and supporters are buried in the last and deepest ditch that can be dug for them, and where they will never have a resurrection!

These loyal citizens have been just as largely interterested in, and benefited by slavery as any others, and vastly more so than thousands of the foolish humbugs who have taken up arms against their flag; but, from the firing of the first gun, they have had common sense enough to see that the "peculiar institution" was doomed, and that slavery—as the boys would say—was a "bad egg." They rejoice with us that an eternal *quietus* is about to be given to the "vexed question," and are rapidly adapting themselves to the new order of things, which has recently taken place in the State of Louisiana. Nay, more, they heartily wish that the course pursued here may be imitated elsewhere, and everywhere throughout the South, until the whole nation, and even the entire American Continent shall be the home of universal freedom.

"God moves," the poet says, "in a mysterious way, his wonders to perform," and out of the mystery of iniquity, in this case, he has brought forth such "wonders," as proclaim his hand, and reveal his power, and wisdom, and goodness, too, in the overthrow of this great wrong and sin in this land.

Soon we can sing, and say, "Hail Columbia!" without the remembrance of that sad and harrowing history of chains and fetters which has been clanking their discord so long.

On the memorable day when the city capitulated to General Butler, and the dear old flag was again spread to the sunlight, from the topmost elevation of the public buildings, a certain gentleman, a minister of the gospel, called all his slaves around him and said, "You are all free now, and I thank God for it." Like a sensible, Christian man, he read the determination of events, and accepted the issue under the providence of God. He saw plainly that with the success of the armies of the Union, slavery became a dead letter, and must go down to the shades of oblivion. The conviction and hope among these Southern patriots, is, that with the removal of this curse, their fair and fertile land will rise to a degree of greatness, power, and prosperity, far beyond anything recorded in her former history. With the passing away of darkness will break a morning of light and a day of joy. Barbarism will yield to humane laws, and ignorance will be replaced with the spread of knowledge, and the foundations of society, instead of idleness and vice, will find a firm basis on the eternal rock of *truth* and *freedom*.

CHAPTER XX.

OBSERVATIONS CONTINUED.

UNMANLY SUBSERVIENCY TO REBELS—FAITHLESS OFFICIALS—CORRUPTION OF PARTIES IN POWER—UNION MEN NEGLECTED—GENERAL CANBY—PROSPECT OF CORRECTING ABUSES.

CONSIDERATION shown to a vanquished foe, when it springs from pure and lofty motives, is noble and commendable; but to see union men, who are identified with the purest cause, in defense of which the sword was ever drawn, doing all in their power to obtain a nod of recognition from some haughty rebel, who has only been able to retain his wealth by adding perjury to treason, is indeed heart-sickening to an independent and honorable man. Yet in this city such a thing is almost of everyday occurrence. Within the inner-chambers of certain officers, in the military and civil departments connected with the government of the United States, scenes are enacted which ought to make those subordinates, clothed with a little brief authority, blush for their manliness.

Even those of higher grade, to whom we might reasonably look for firmness, competency, and unbending loyalty, are often found uniting in an unholy alliance with the former, to promote the interests and shield the persons of notorious rebels, by procuring for them lucrative offices and profitable contracts, while the modest applications of true union men for office or employment are treated with supercilious neglect, and totally disregarded. Is this right? is it just? In imagination I seem to hear the united voice of millions of true-hearted men, in thunder-tones, answer—No!

There are at the present time in this city well-known persons, who have been in the rebel army, who are making immense sums of money out of positions given them under the government.

I have been informed that some of these office-holders were imprisoned by General Butler for their open, undisguised treason, but released by the authorities subsequently, and actually admitted to intimacy and fellowship with certain parties high in power, who have strangely overlooked their duty in elevating such persons to the dignity and responsibilities of a share in the government they tried to rend and destroy. Verily, "Consistency, thou art a jewel." It is strongly suspected that some of our government officials favor these men with the understanding that they pocket a large per-centage of their gains. Under such a state of affairs good men have but small chance for justice. If they make complaints they endanger their own liberty, property, and even life, and consequently must endure, in silence and sadness, the rule of unrighteousness, hoping for better days.

General Canby, who has recently assumed command of this department, is a man who will look sharply into these abuses, and, with a strong and impartial hand, correct those which are known to exist. Under his administration there is a prospect of securing right and justice to all, and of bringing the guilty to merited punishment.

CHAPTER XXI.

OBSERVATIONS CONTINUED.

SCENES AND INCIDENTS—COFFEE-HOUSES—A DISAPPOINTED MAJOR—A WOODEN-LEGGED HERO, AND ONE-ARMED "REB"—A LOST BOY TURNS UP—OPINION OF AN EX-SLAVEHOLDER—THE PATRIOTISM OF A COLOR SERGEANT—SACRIFICES FOR COUNTRY—"THE WRONG BOAT"—ALGIERS M. E. CHURCH—SUNDAY SCHOOL.

"COFFEE-HOUSES," as I have heretofore stated, abound in this city, but the kind of beverage furnished on demand within their precincts, is not invariably the extract of "Rio." A Major of our army, one day, attracted by the sign, walked into one of these places, and ordered a cup of coffee. The proprietor, a genuine Dutchman, replied that he could give him a glass of whisky, but the other article was not in his line. The Major looked him sternly in the eye, and inquired, "Is not this a coffee-house?" The Teuton said that was only its name, the real intent being a place to obtain "bitters," "slings," "cocktails," and "mint-juleps."

The Major, thus enlightened, took his departure, a wiser man, not knowing before, that all the whisky shops, even down to the lowest hell-hole, adopt the decent name and character of a "Coffee-house."

Instances of true heroism among our private soldiers

have not been rare. I saw one of these veterans one day engaged in an exciting dispute with a returned rebel soldier. The Federal had a wooden leg, and the other an empty sleeve. I suppose they had been comparing notes, and split on the merits of the main question. The man with but one leg, was holding forth in an eloquent, patriotic strain, and said, "Yes, *Sir*, I lost that leg in fighting for my country, a glorious cause, no need to be ashamed of a wooden leg, in place of the old one shot away. Yes, I am willing to fight on until the other one goes, and then my right arm, and after that my left arm, and will give my life, if necessary, to crush this d——d rebellion."

The "Reb" was silenced, and slunk away, apparently ashamed that the scar *he* bore was not an honorable one, but would be to him and his posterity a lasting disgrace.

In the hospital I had charge of, there was a little English boy, who ran away from his home in Canada, soon after the breaking out of hostilities. His parents, not hearing from him for a long period, and having no knowledge where he had gone, gave him up as lost. News was sent to them of his whereabouts, to their great delight. He had been in our army, and unlike many of his countrymen, who did all they could to widen the breach, and encourage the rebellion, he espoused our cause, and gave all his service for the honor of his adopted country's flag, and the putting down of this wicked resistance to the government.

I listened to a conversation one day, between two ex-slaveholders, on the state of the country. One of them remarked to the other, that the time would come, in the history of Louisiana, when her soil would be tilled by more than ten thousand Irishmen, and that he believed the free-labor system would bring about a degree of unexampled greatness and prosperity, when it should be introduced and generally adopted.

This man entertained a correct view of the situation, and I have no doubt at all, but it will be more than realized, if events are allowed to pursue their pathway, unobstructed by sectional prejudice, or that narrow policy, which sometimes, as the adage says, "cuts off one's nose to spite the face."

Benjamin Franklin Walls was color-sergeant of the Fifty-sixth Pennsylvania Volunteers, and was for several weeks a patient in the St. James' Hospital. He had been in the field nearly three years, having joined our forces from Cumberland Valley, Pa., his native place. He brought in forty men, recruited through his influence when he enlisted. This entitled him to a captaincy, but he declined that position, declaring that he aspired to no higher honor than to carry the flag of his country, for which his father fought before him in the last war with England. The honor was cheerfully conferred on him, and through six severe battles he bore it in triumph and with alacrity, although he was over sixty years of age. While he was in the Hospital the surgeon offered to procure for him an honorable discharge, in view of his sickness and advanced age. This he refused to accept, preferring to return with his brave comrades in arms at the end of the war, and bear his beloved banner back untarnished to the Keystone State. Pennsylvania may justly feel proud of such a son; yet he is but the type of thousands, who for the integrity and unity of this great nation gave up lucrative employments, bid adieu to home comforts, and bravely fought, and many of them alas! nobly fell with their face to the foe. Sergeant Walls was worth when he entered the service about one hundred thousand dollars, but patriotism was with him a stronger passion than the pursuit or care of wealth. May he, and all who like him have given such evidence of devotion to the stars and stripes be spared to a green and happy old age, and dying at last,

> "As sleep the brave who sink to rest
> By all their country's wishes blest,"

may they find a rich reward in the bosom of their God.

On account of the scarcity of Union ministers in the city and its surroundings, I had to take pastoral charge of the M. E. Church in Algiers, just across the river from New Orleans. The duties involved in this charge, added to those connected with my Hospital, made my life a somewhat busy one. Hundreds of times I have crossed the Mississippi in going to and from my church. Most of the people among whom I mingled being in bitter hostility to the Union, my experience was a varied one. Between insults, provocation, and not unfrequently amusing incidents, I tried to discharge with fidelity the trust committed to my care. During an extra meeting I held there, large numbers of secessionists attended. Some of them had the assurance to walk up and take the front seats in the church, refusing to kneel in time of prayer, besides disturbing the meeting by laughing and talking. This did not continue very long before they found out that they were "aboard of the wrong boat." I compelled them not only to behave with becoming decorum, but also to conform to our usage by kneeling during prayer, or else leave the church. I could not reconcile it with my sense of the fitness of things to allow these votaries of Jeff. Davis and zealous friends of his arch instigator with the horns and cloven foot from below, to disturb and interrupt loyal people while worshipping the living God.

My relation as Sunday School Superintendent was quite interesting and pleasant, as but few of the children in attendance manifested a spirit of stubborn disloyalty. When I referred to subjects connected with the war for the Union, and required obedience to the "powers that be," it did not seem to offend them, thus showing that they had better sense and more love of country, than their parents.

CHAPTER XXII.

OBSERVATIONS CONTINUED.

METHODIST SOLDIERS—TESTIMONY TO THEIR RELIGIOUS ZEAL—THE SOURCE OF POWER—A PREMIUM ON DISLOYALTY—CONTRABAND TRAFFIC—BACK-DOOR BUSINESS—SCENE IN A CHURCH.

DURING my term of service as Chaplain in the Army of the Potomac, I found it invariably the case that the soldiers on whom I could rely with most confidence for help in carrying on prayer-meetings, were mostly members of the Methodist Episcopal Church, and not a few Chaplains of other denominations have admitted the same thing to be true in their experience. I have also been told by agents of the Christian Commission that the Methodist soldiers were of more practical service to them in their religious operations than any, and all others combined. Hospital Chaplains, also, have stated to me the same fact. The reason of this, evidently is, that it forms a prominent part of the teaching and training of this Church, to make all its members do their own praying, and not rely on those of others—even the minister, for help in the time of need. Learning thus to pray at home, they find it easy to pray abroad, to pray anywhere, and to "pray without ceasing."

Every Church, I think should aim, to stir up the gifts

and bring out the talents of all its members, in the manner peculiar to Methodism, and then there would be more useful Christians in the world. The "burning and shining lights" would appear everywhere, flashing condemnation in the face of all sin, and showing wanderers the path to heaven.

Many, I might say, *most* of those now in the ranks of the Methodist ministry, men of acknowledged talent and power, were it not for the active system of mutual labor to which they were inured when young in the kingdom, would to-day be in the back ground, and perhaps not on "the walls of Zion," proclaiming salvation.

Everything appertaining to the welfare and honor of this denomination, of which I am happy to be a member and minister, is of deepest interest to me. Hence the facts I have gathered, and here record as a memorial of worth, energy, and spirituality, according to the testimony from many sources of our God-appointed Methodism. No other Church in this land has been taxed so heavily for soldiers to recruit the ranks of our armies, and yet, no other Church has been so studiously overlooked, or neglected, in the bestowment of government patronage. The Episcopal, and Roman Catholic Churches, known to be less loyal, seem to have far more influence at head-quarters, in securing good positions for their members as officers and Chaplains, than any other. This would seem to put a premium on disloyalty, and reward the lukewarm, while the earnest and faithful, who have borne the heat and burden of the war, are left to feel aggrieved if they choose, or take what others may relinquish, in the way of subordinate appointments. On history, mainly, however, we must rely for the justice which, I feel free to say, has not been meted out to us. Posterity will duly estimate our claims, and not let the remembrance of our labors perish.

Many attempts have been made on the part of the government to stop contraband trading with the enemy, but thus far without success: for, as the business is carried on in an indirect way on the back-door principle, and the gains on cotton and tobacco are considerable, money outweighs patriotism, and the love of it, with many, is a stronger passion than either honor, fear, or loyalty. It is strongly suspected that this extensive intercourse with the rebels would not, or could not be carried on successfully, were it not that many in the employ of the government, in a secret way give encouragement to those known to be engaged in this species of trade by shielding them from arrest, and sharing in the profits, which are extraordinary, on the capital invested.

During my pastorate at Algiers, an incident occurred, quite in character with the general spirit of the leading citizens. On a certain Sabbath morning, after preaching in the M. E. Church, a colored child was brought forward for baptism. When the minister began the ceremony, three of the male members arose, and in a very abrupt and insulting manner left the house, declaring they would never enter its door again. The subject for baptism was certainly a proper one, and the rite was administered with all due decency and solemnity, but these hot-headed followers of Jesus (!) were offended, like the mistaken disciples of old, their chief cause of complaint was the undue prominence given to a mere "nigger." Can such enter the kingdom of heaven? One of the three repented of his folly and returned—the other two hold out faithful to "southern rights," and doubtless are still on the road to the Devil.

CHAPTER XXIII.

OBSERVATIONS CONTINUED.

OFFICERS' GENERAL HOSPITAL—ST. JAMES' HOTEL—CAPACITY—SURGEONS—EXPERIENCE WITH THE SICK AND WOUNDED—TESTIMONY OF THE DYING—CAPTAIN YOUNG, &c.—CHAPLAINS.

THE hospital to which I have occasion so frequently to refer, called St. James', and in which my duties chiefly lay, was devoted to officers, and very finely arranged and located for the purpose to which it was devoted by the military authorities. Before the war it was used as a first class hotel. It stands on Magazine St., in the business portion of the city, and contains one hundred and seventy-five lodging-rooms, with ample parlor accommodations. It is five stories high, with ornamental front, and very imposing appearance. The government pays ten thousand dollars a year for the use of it. This officers' general hospital is under the charge of Surgeon S. M. Horton, of the regular army. He is a Pennsylvanian, and the old Keystone commonwealth has no reason to be ashamed of him. He is not only an honor to his native State, but to the entire country. His assistants are Dr. H. C. Heilner and Dr. S. Catlin. The former is also a Pennsylvanian, and is a young man of great promise, reflecting honor on the Jefferson Medical College, where he graduated quite young, and with very marked distinction. Dr. Catlin is a man of fine ability, and stands deservedly high in his profession. With these three gentlemen I was happy to be associated, and cannot forget the kind consideration extended to me by each to facilitate the performance of my duties.

Many of the inmates of this establishment were men of refined intelligence and high position both in civil and military life. Broken down in health, or severely wounded in battle, they were brought here for care and treatment, and made as comfortable as possible under the circumstances. Some within these walls exchanged earth for heaven. I have witnessed many scenes of holy triumph among them in the dying hour. Christianity is a soul-satisfying portion, when "sickness, sorrow, pain, or death" is felt and realized. I will attempt to recal a few particulars in relation to those on whom I was permitted and privileged to attend in their last hours.

Captain William E. Young was the son of ex-Governor Young, of New York. He belonged to the corps of topographical engineers, and was on the staff of General Banks. He was not only a skilful officer, and highly valuable in the branch of service to which he was attached, but was brave and adventurous wherever the post of duty and danger was found. He never seemed to calculate results of exposure in undertakings of great peril. At the battle of Cane River, he volunteered to convey despatches of an important character to a particular point, and in the performance of this duty was frightfully wounded. He lingered about five weeks, and was in the full possession of all his faculties up to the time of his death. He took a decided interest in religious exercises, and professed conversion to God while I was engaged in singing and prayer with him. For five weeks I visited him every day, and always found him in a happy frame of mind, relying on God, through the merits of Jesus Christ, for acceptance and salvation. Frequently I have known him to break forth in songs of praise and holy joy. He had no fear of dying, and as the hour approached, he said to me, "Chaplain, tell my mother that God is with me." This was his last message to his mother, who no doubt will derive comfort from the knowledge that, although away from home, her son died in the glorious hope of a home in heaven. His funeral took place from the Carondolet St. Methodist church, and was attended by Rev. Dr. Newman and several other prominent clergymen, with myself, showing the esteem in which this brave young officer was held by all who knew him.

Chaplain Keely, of the Thirteenth Maine, departed this life on the 25th of June, 1864. As the last moment approached, a sweet smile of heavenly triumph lit up his countenance, and gave assurance to all around that "he feared no evil" in the dark valley. His affectionate son, Lieutenant Keely, was by his side day and night, watching over him with true filial tenderness as a guardian angel, until the sad task alone remained to close the eyes of that beloved father in the sleep of death. If kindness and constancy is rewarded on earth, that son will surely prosper on account of his devotion to a sick and dying father, who has gone from labor to reward.

Chaplain Dwyer, of the Second New York Veteran Regiment, died in great peace on Wednesday morning, June 29th, 1864. He was a very fine Christian gentleman, and was very favorably known to several of the Chaplains in and around the city, as a devoted servant of God.

I am not prepared to believe the libels of many abusive and drunken Congressmen and others who have from time to time cast slurs, and sneering misrepresentations upon the character, piety, and disinterested zeal of the Chaplains; for I have found them, both in the Army of the Potomac, and in the Department of the Gulf, to be an intelligent, pious, and singularly excellent and faithful body of men; serving God and their generation with a single eye to his glory, and the welfare of immortal souls.

I have had as many as six Chaplains under my care, in the Hospital at one time, and always found them consistent and true to their sacred calling.

Corporal Casey, of the Sixty-seventh Indiana Regiment, is another example of the power of faith and sustaining grace in a dying hour. He had for years been a devoted member of the M. E. Church, and therefore when he fell covered with wounds, he knew Him whom he had believed, and was resigned to the will of the Lord. His sufferings were intense, but his fortitude, cheerfulness, and Christian hope never forsook him. His last message to his wife and children, was, to meet him in heaven, each, and all, in the bright and happy land, where pain, and parting tears shall come no more forever. Oh, that my last end may be like his.

In conclusion, I humbly thank God for the degree of success which attended my labors in this Hospital. Many, very many, I saw happily converted, some of whom afterwards died shouting victory through the blood of the Lamb.

CHAPTER XXIV.

OBSERVATIONS CONTINUED.

"THE PATRIOT'S CEMETERY"—WISDOM OF GENERAL BUTLER—MY COUSIN THOMAS D. GREGG—CHALMETTE BATTLE-GROUND—MONUMENT CEMETERY—THE MANTLE OF "OLD HICKORY"—FARRAGUT AND BUTLER—GOD FOR THE CAUSE OF LIBERTY—THE SOLDIERS' LAST RESTING-PLACE.

A MELANCHOLY interest will ever linger round the places where our brave men lie buried in the south, who fell in battle, or wasted away in weary marches, and gave their precious lives for country and liberty.

Nearly four thousand men, who once in all the pride of health and patriotism, stepped forth to the music of the Union, sleep their last sleep in Grove Cemetery near New Orleans. This resting-place of the dead is located at Metaire Ridge, a distance of three miles from the city. Its selection as a burying-ground for our soldiers was one of those clear indications of the excellent judgment of General Butler. He had a portion of the grounds neatly fenced in, and a magnificent arch constructed over the entrance, surmounted by an American eagle, and flag-staff bearing aloft the banner so dear to the soldier of the Union, and wrapped in the folds of which his comrades bore his body to this beautiful spot for military

A Soldier's last resting place.

Life in the Army, p. 198.

interment. Inscribed upon the arch may be read in legible characters "THE PATRIOT'S CEMETERY."

Within this enclosure rested for a time the body of Thomas D. Gregg, a cousin to the writer. He belonged to the First Delaware Battery, and was a very promising young man, possessing many noble qualities of mind and heart. He owned a fine farm near Wilmington, Delaware, at the time of his death. This property has remained in our name for over one hundred and forty years. His remains have been removed to his native home, and now sleep side by side with his parents and friends near Wilmington.

Chalmette battle-ground is celebrated in history as being the place where General Jackson defeated the British under Gibbs and Packenham, in 1814. It is located six miles below the city, on the west bank of the great river. Since the 6th of May, 1864, this notable spot has been chosen as a burying-place for our soldiers, by the military authorities, and is now used for this purpose. It is called "Monument Cemetery." The site is all that could be desired, both on account of its historic interest and favorable location. An unfinished monument is erected there to the memory of the conqueror and hero, General Jackson.

The rebels had thrown up extensive breastworks there, intending to make a stand against our forces approaching the city. They were no doubt inspired with some vague notion that the spirit of the old General, and the help of God might aid them in keeping the Union army at bay

But both resources failed them, and they ignominiously fled, thinking it best to cave in, and capitulate, as they were on the wrong side this time. If the spirit and mantle of "Old Hickory" was there at all, it must have rested on the invincible Farragut, and his brave coadjutor Butler, as they battered to the dust the flag and forts of traitors, and thundered up the river the memorable words in smoke and flame, "*The Union it must and shall be preserved.*"

The bodies of our deceased soldiers, are now conveyed to Monument Cemetery, by a small steamer plying twice a day, and chartered for this exclusive purpose. I have attended the funeral of as many as thirty-three in one day at that locality, and every one of them, as I suppose, leaving a sad gap, not only in the ranks they were proud to fill, but in home circles far away. Oh! how many hearts bleed for those who shall return no more.

May the great Physician be present to heal the sorrows of the wife bereaved, the mother in mourning, and the children, robbed by this cruel and relentless war, of the counsel and care of a beloved father.

Time, and the nation's sympathy will do much to soften and soothe the hard lot of those left desolate. Time will make the grass green above the single grave or mound where no battle sound can again reach the ear of the fallen: and a redeemed nation will gratefully cherish the memory of every soldier, who on its altar laid down his life, that children's children might enjoy the birthright and blessing of free government for ever.

CHAPTER XXV.

OBSERVATIONS CONTINUED.

TAXABLE PROPERTY—WEALTH OF THE COLORED PEOPLE—THEIR PIETY—POWER IN PRAYER—THEIR "MOSES"—DENOMINATIONS—LARGE SECESSION FROM THE CHURCH SOUTH—ADMIXTURE OF RACES—WRONGS ENDURED—A REMARKABLE WEDDING—FATHER ROSS—THE GREAT EMANCIPATION CELEBRATION—THE MILITARY—PRAYER AND ORATIONS—IMMENSE PARADE—SONG BY THE CHILDREN—THE FIRST COLORED REGIMENT—A SCRAP OF HISTORY—THE ORGANIZATION OF COLORED TROOPS—THEIR ADAPTATION TO CLIMATE, DRILL, AND DISCIPLINE—THEIR VICTORIES—EQUAL RIGHTS—THE NATION'S DUTY TO THE COLORED MAN.

THE amount of taxable property in this city before the war was one hundred and four millions, of which the colored people owned, and paid taxes on *fifteen millions of dollars!* Who would have supposed this?

The colored population is estimated at forty thousand souls, and many among them are intelligent, influential, and wealthy people. As a class, they are noted for good morals, and in general character and conduct, are examples of uprightness.

Some of them are the finest-looking colored people I ever saw. About two-thirds speak the English language, and the balance, the French, Spanish, and Italian. They publish a daily, and a tri-weekly newspaper, in the French and English languages, called the "New Orleans Tribune," which has quite a large circulation. The majority are attached to the Protestant faith, and a large proportion of them are Methodists. They have four Methodist churches in the city, which, until recently, were connected with the church south. About three thousand of their number have attached themselves to us, and are now included in the old loyal and anti-slavery church of our fathers, under the general oversight of the Rev. Dr. Newman.

They were glad of the opportunity to renounce the southern branch of the Church, and show their love for true Methodism and their loyalty to the government by coming over to us. There are three African and four Baptist churches, also sustained by them, in the city, and two hundred and thirty schools, now under their own control, in the state.

No fact is more fully established at present than that of the true, hearty, and unfaltering devotion of the southern colored people to the union. Everywhere they have given unquestioned evidence of their sincere patriotism. Without their information and guidance many a campaign would have closed without success, many a union prisoner would have pined and died in hopeless dungeons, and many a dangerous rebel would have continued secretly to ply his wicked work of opposition to the lawful authorities.

They are, moreover, among the most devout, God-fearing, and faithful Christians, according to their light and opportunities, which this nation, or any other, has known. They are a people of prayer, of patience under provocation, of meekness in suffering, and, as a general thing, consistent in character, with the strictest rules of Church discipline.

In New Orleans it is a rare sight to see a colored person in the hands of a civil officer, and never, in all my experience, have I seen one of them on the street drunk. They are sober, industrious, and economical, supporting themselves out of their own earnings, and dividing, with generous liberality, their substance for the maintenance of their own poor and the cause of religion. It is a great error to suppose that the government is burdened with their support. Only a few of the old and helpless, who have been turned adrift upon the world, need the care and rations of the commissary department.

Whatever is done for them in this way is appreciated with sincere thankfulness, while thousands of the impoverished whites, who have become pensioners on the bounty of the government, actually curse the hand that supplies their daily wants, and sneer at those who keep them from starving.

The name of President Lincoln was their strong tower, and tens of thousands among them sent up their prayers to heaven for blessings on his head. He stood before them, as Moses did among the Israelites in former days, and if earnest love and incessant supplication ever helped a man to heaven, the martyred president is surely near the throne. Who, that believes his Bible, can doubt but that this oppressed people have power with God, and that the wondrous results of these days, shaped, as they are, by an unseen and Almighty arm, are the answers to a century of groans and crying.

Among the wrongs endured by these poor, defenseless people, perhaps the greatest and most cruel is that which ignores virtue and chastity, and has, up to this time, violated all the sacredness of the "holy estate of matrimony" among them. The southern people are the very last in the world who ought to cry out against amalgamation. The evidences are all around you here of the extent to which this practice has been carried. Look at a few facts bearing practically on this question. According to general report the "mulatto" is one half white blood, the "quadroon" one fourth negro, and the "octoroon" one eighth.

A very large proportion of the entire colored population, belong to one or other of these classes, and a genuine African, is more of an exception than the rule in this city. Many of the "octoroons," are so white, that you can scarcely distinguish them from their white fathers! yes, fathers who held them in bondage, and sold them like cattle! But the days of the auction block are past and gone, never to return; and for this every humane heart in the nation ought to sing the doxology at least once a day.

Six years of my life have been spent in southern states, during which time I have observed the cruel treatment of masters, mistresses, overseers, and in fact, nearly everybody else resident there toward the poor slave. I have heard them cursed on every hand, and seen them whipped, sold, and treated in the most inhuman manner.

I have seen the gallery-doors of a church I once built in Maryland locked against them, as if they were unfit to enter the same building with white people, to worship God together, as if the negro had no soul, or was of an entirely different order of creation. I do not remember ever to have heard one, even of the most pious masters invite them into family-worship, or impress upon them the propriety of attending church. It is now the oft repeated cry, that they are unfit for freedom, and should still be kept in the back ground, as it regards education, and the means of moral and religious improvement. Who are to blame if the colored man is in ignorance, and deficient in almost every element of social life? How can it be expected that he would be otherwise kept so long in degradation and infancy, as to all the great purposes of manhood? Let him have even half a chance, and in education, enterprise, and social position, he will work out his own salvation, and earn the right to any privilege accorded to a free American citizen. The prejudice against caste or color will melt away like the morning mist, and will only be remembered in the future as an unreasonable, and unchristian feeling, founded on wrong principles, and fostered only as a relic of barbarism.

Many scenes occurred under my notice, in this city,

which I could attribute only to empty-headed ignorance, or rebel spite. Ladies frequently visited the cemetery, and would linger among the graves of traitors, while I have known them to shun that part of the grounds where some of our brave colored soldiers lie buried.

Living or dying, or even dead, these secessionists hate all who have enrolled themselves under the flag of the free, to battle for the right, and save, for after generations an undivided nationality.

There are nine military schools for the instruction of colored children within the limits of the city, with an average attendance of two thousand, four hundred eager pupils, all alive to the importance of education. The "American Missionary Association," has about twenty teachers in this department, some of whom are connected with colored regiments, giving at every leisure moment instructions to the men, many of whom are apt learners, and are rapidly advancing to that degree of proficiency, in which they will be able to read the Bible and the Constitution, a thing which thousands of the white population have not yet attained to and never will.

This association has also a Sunday-school under its control, numbering about six hundred scholars.

I attended a remarkable wedding, which took plaee one evening in St. Paul's colored M. E. church. "Father Ross," the venerable preacher in charge, first held a short prayer-meeting, and then put on his spectacles, and with book in hand, came down from the pulpit, and standing at the altar railing, he ordered, in a commanding tone of voice, the parties who were present to be married, to come at once forward. At this moment all the official members arose and took their places on the right and left of the officiating minister.

The couple also presented themselves in front, and the ceremony proceeded. After the usual questions were asked, the bridegroom gave assent by nodding his head. This, however, did not satisfy Father Ross. He cried out sternly, "'*I will*' is the answer!" and insisted on both giving audible responses. When the ceremony was concluded, the old minister commanded the already frightened bridegroom to kiss his bride, which he proceeded to do in such a style as to produce a general smile among the lookers on.

I had heard of such a custom as this before, and suppose it is an importation from some parts of Europe, but never witnessed the practical operation of it, except on this occasion. It seemed to me, that before a large assembly, especially, this salutation, as the finale of the marriage rite, would be more highly "honored in the breach than in the observance."

The 11th of June, 1864, was a high day at Congo Square. It was the celebration of the Emancipation Proclamation, and was an occasion of thrilling interest. Many a secessionist in anticipation had prayed that the day might be rainy, or otherwise unfavorable; but in this, as in numerous other instances, the Good Being did not, or would not, hearken and grant the request of traitors, and the weather was most propitious. A number of colored regiments, with burnished steel and banners flying, took part in the parade, and then formed into a hollow square, encircling the large platform, which was most appropriately decorated. These soldiers, in their bearing and precision of movement, made a very fine appearance, and contributed greatly to the imposing ceremonies of the occasion.

The music was soul-stirring, and touched the heart-strings of twenty thousand people, old and young, making them vibrate with the highest feelings of thankfulness and joy.

After the meeting was called to order, one of the colored clergymen present offered a most eloquent and impressive prayer to the Almighty, in which he thanked God that they as a people were permitted to witness this day of jubilee, the greatest, the brightest, the best day they had ever seen. They had prayed for it, and waited long in hope, and now, said he, "O God, roll on the tide of freedom, until every slave in the whole land is, as many here are to-day; until the oppressed everywhere shall rejoice in possession of liberty. O Lord, bless General Banks, and may he continue to shed light on us poor colored people. Father in heaven, bless General Butler. We thank thee that thou didst ever send him along this way. Bless him now, at the head of his army, and may it be in thy good providence that he shall soon return to us here again. O our God and King, bless the great Union army and navy with courage and success, until our flag shall cover the earth as the waters cover the great and mighty sea. May the 'Star-spangled Banner' soon become the acknowledged flag of the wide-spread earth! O God, bless to-day thy servant, our chief executive, the President of these United States, and make this nation the greatest empire on the face of the globe."

At the conclusion of the prayer, the throng of colored people raised a general cheer, moved to this expression of their appreciation, I suppose, by its solid ring of loyalty.

I noticed among other distinguished persons present Major-General Banks, Governor Hahn, Rev. Mr. Gilbert, Rev. Mr. Bass, and Rev. C. Strong.

There were two very able addresses delivered, one in English and the other in French by colored orators, and from the eager and undivided attention given to their words, and the tremendous applause which greeted them, I should think the effort of each was a grand success.

Governor Hahn also made a brief, and very telling speech, which was enthusiastically received.

The following is one of the songs which was sung on the occasion, and which produced a great effect. It was sung by the colored Sabbath School children, under the leadership of the gentlemanly and efficient Chaplain Conaway, who has bestowed a large amount of attention on their training in morals, religion, and correct views of government:

SONG

IN HONOR OF EMANCIPATION.

AIR—" *Our Little Meeting,*" Native Melody.

Slavery's chain is bound to break,
Slavery's chain is bound to break,
Slavery's chain is bound to break,
And Massa and I must part—
So fare you well poor massa;
May God Almighty help you,
I'll never feel your lash again,
For Freedom's got the start!

Our ransomed race is bound to take,
Our ransomed race is bound to take,
Our ransomed race is bound to take
The road that leads to light.
So fare you well, poor massa,
May God Almighty help you;
I'll never feel your lash agaln,
For God is with the right!

Louisiana's star is shining bright,
GENERAL BANKS is giving light,
Our Convention is doing right,
And now we all are free.
So fare you well, poor massa,
May God Almighty help you;
I'll never feel your lash again,
For now we all are free!

At the close of the interesting exercises in the square, the large concourse of people, including the military, and accompanied with music, paraded through the principal streets, and then broke up without disorder. The whole affäir was a novel spectacle and a grand success.

It may surprise some to hear that up to this time there have been twelve thousand seven hundred colored soldiers recruited in this department, and all of them that I have seen under arms make a very fine appearance. Their general conduct is said to be excellent, and no doubt need be entertained of their bravery under fire. History will record its testimony on this point.

It is claimed that the very first colored regiment enlisted in the United States service was formed here by order of Major-General Butler, who assumed the responsibility, and called the troops by the name of "the Native Home Guard," reminding the astonished and disgusted chivalry of a scrap of history which, perhaps, they had forgotten, viz, that both General Washington in the Revolution, and General Jackson in the last war with Great Britain, enrolled colored soldiers in the ranks of the American army. We all remember with what intense earnestness the rebels and their Northern allies plead and protested against making the colored man a soldier. It was argued that the white troops would not bear the infliction of such disgrace as this arrangement contemplated to them—that they would leave the service *en masse* if required to fight alongside of the negro, and that it was a waste of time and energy to undertake the drill, discipline, and command of colored regiments; for they would run at the first fire, and would prove incompetent in every quality of a good soldier. All this was urged time and again; but the government in the hands of such men as the now revered Lincoln, and the inflexible Secretary Stanton, persevered, and what are the facts: the world knows their proud record of endurance, bravery, discipline, and success, when, and wherever the order has been "forward." The wisdom of recruiting them by tens of thousands is now vindicated by their adaptation to service in the Southern climate, and their perfect subordination when fairly used and properly paid. Yes, they have not only helped to conquer the rebels and carry the flag of the free in triumph over the territory where they were denied even the rights of manhood; but they have won for themselves the respect and regard of the nation. They have conquered an enemy almost as formidable as the rebellion itself, that is, the prejudice which everywhere met them, and paralyzed their efforts at self-elevation and social improvement.

Whatever my judgment is worth, I give it, that the hand which lays down the rifle, with the return of peace has earned the privilege to deposit a ballot, and while thousands of the time-serving trimmers of the border states, and the actually disloyal, north and south, who have tried to destroy this government, should be forever disqualified for part or participation in the elective franchise, the good, honest, loyal, intelligent colored man, should be recognized as a citizen, and enjoy the most perfect equality before the law. It should be the duty of the general, and state governments, as well as of the intelligent and humane everywhere to reach forth a helping hand, and lift him up.

Christianity too, in all its noble dictates, requires us to overcome the trivial, and unreasonable antipathies, which too long have been allowed to alienate the strong from this weaker portion of the great family of one Almighty Father, and give the gospel, with a free, unsparing liberality to those who have been suddenly disenthralled, and cast upon the sympathies of those who profess to love the Lord Jesus Christ. My heart's desire and prayer to God for this people is, that they may be brought to the knowledge of salvation, and made a peculiar people in holiness, and zealous of good works.

CHAPTER XXVI.

OBSERVATIONS CONTINUED.

REV. J. P. NEWMAN, D.D.—POSITION AND INFLUENCE—AN OLD LADY'S PRAYER—UNCLE SAM, THE GREATEST PRESIDENT—ALL SAINTS' DAY—BURYING ABOVE GROUND—CLIMATE—YOUNG AMERICA—IGNORANCE OF SOME OF THE COLORED PEOPLE—SINGULAR NAMES—THE MARRYING BUSINESS—CHRISTMAS—SABBATH SCHOOL EXHIBITIONS—WATCH NIGHT—LAZY METHODISTS—A DAY OF JUBILEE—THE CHRISTIAN AND SANITARY COMMISSIONS—STEAMBOAT COLLISIONS—THE CITY AS A MILITARY CAMP—THREE THOUSAND COLORED CHILDREN AT THE CIRCUS—A RAID ON THE GAMBLING-HOUSES—SABBATH DESECRATION PREVENTED—ANNIVERSARY OF THE BATTLE OF NEW ORLEANS—INAUGURATION OF GOVERNOR WELLS—GREAT TURN OUT OF THE FIRE DEPARTMENT—ELOQUENT PRAYER—A MEMORABLE DAY—VALUABLE SERVICES OF DR. J. V. E. SMITH—THE ROLL OF HONOR.

MY residence in New Orleans, brought me in contact with many persons, and peculiarities in social and official life, which demanded a few paragraphs, descriptive and explanatory, for the information or amusement of those who may be pleased to read these pages.

With all the incidents of an active round of duties, and the novelty to me of various customs and habits among the people, I think, my stay would have been much more dreary, and my position far less agreeable, had I not formed the acquaintance, and experienced the friendship, counsel, and Christian regard of a gentleman, to whose name I cannot give too prominent a place, either in my book, or heart's best esteem. Let me introduce him as

THE REV. J. P. NEWMAN, D.D.

The appointment of Dr. Newman as a superintendent of the mission work of the Methodist Episcopal Church in this department, reflects the highest honor on the judgment and sagacity of our excellent Bishop Ames. And that the Doctor himself should consent to exile from the more congenial associations of his northern home, to face and grapple with the difficulties involved, is greatly to his credit and character, as a self-sacrificing minister of Jesus.

Ever since his arrival, the whole community have felt the force of his eloquence, and the cause of God and his country has realized signal advantage from his timely counsels and faithful ministrations.

In the pulpit and prayer-meeting, and on the platform, his ability, genius, and intense devotion, have shone out as a light in darkness, and no man in this city occupies to-day a more influential position than he. How he manages so much work, is a mystery, but here he is, one hour leading a class, the next perhaps closeted with a commander of the army, or familiar with the deliberations of municipal officers, or called to give his views on grave matters of state policy, and then, off to some remote point to meet another engagement growing out of his complicated and responsible task.

He boldly tears the mask from vice, exposes rascality in every form, and is the champion of virtue, right, and true religion, making the press, as well as the rostrum tributary to this great end, and in the work of conversion, he aims not only to bring sinners to God, but out of all treasonable sentiments to earnest loyalty. He has been largely blessed with success in his protracted meetings, and honored by a precious revival. His course of sermons to young men were attractive, convincing, and masterly discourses, and his "half-hour" sermons to the people, drew crowds to the house of prayer. Not unfrequently you might there see a Major-General seated side by side with a private soldier, listening to the word of life and salvation. The Doctor is *the* man for such an important outpost of Zion, and will be an honor to the church he represents, as long as it may please God to spare his valuable life.

AN OLD SECESH LADY

whom Dr. Newman met with one day, while out reconnoitering, with a view to organize a loyal Methodist society, in a village near the city, told him, with great confidence that the south would certainly succeed. "How do you know?" said he. "Because," replied the sister, "I have *prayed* for it!"

"UNCLE SAM" THE GREATEST PRESIDENT.

I heard a colored man declare one day, after hearing of the success of the union army and the progress of emancipation, that, in his opinion, "Uncle Sam" was the greatest president ever elected to the white house.

"ALL SAINTS'" DAY.

The calendar of the Roman Catholic Church, as all are aware, is crowded with "saints'" days, which are observed as religious festivals. The 1st of November is termed "All Saints' day," and was a notable occasion in the city. The previous evening is denominated "Hallow eve," and is a time of great hilarity. On this occasion the relatives of deceased persons visit the grave-yards, and place garlands on the vaults and tombs where the remains of friends are interred. Prayers are offered, also, by the priests, for the dead, on this particular day.

HOMES FOR THE DEAD.

There are a large number of very beautiful and costly monuments and vaults in the different cemeteries in and around the city. These places are kept in very nice order, and are rarely without visitors. All who are able to afford it have the remains of their friends placed in vaults, constructed on the surface of the ground, for the reason that the soil is naturally low and level, and graves dug in it soon become filled with water.

These receptacles are built from five to twenty feet high, and, to a person coming here from the high and rolling lands of the north, they present a curious contrast with the usual order elsewhere.

THE CLIMATE OF NEW ORLEANS.

During the fall season, from the last of September to the first of December, the climate here is as delightful as can well be imagined; but, from December to March, a change occurs which makes a disagreeable interval of the year. A great quantity of rain falls during this season, and the cold is more severe than many in the north suppose. It is necessary to have fire in your dwelling most of the time, and out of doors persons are compelled to move more rapidly, and put on gloves and overcoat to feel comfortable.

The spring is mild and very pleasant. During the months of April and May vegetation reaches an extraordinary state of maturity. Flowers burst into bloom, and fruits develope with tropical rapidity.

I have experienced all the changes of the year, and can testify that in general there is but little danger to health, if prudence and care be exercised in guarding against the effect of sudden transitions in the atmosphere, until a person becomes fully acclimated.

YOUNG AMERICA

is here in all the precocity which has marked his character elsewhere. One fine morning, as I was hurrying along toward the hospital, a very little boy hailed me with the utmost confidence, and asked the favor of a match to light his cigar. He could not have been much over two feet high, and four summers old, and yet he was determined to enjoy his smoke, in imitation of larger folks.

This is but one out of many instances in which I have seen the same trait cropping out as distinctly as it could well be defined among the Yankees down east.

LAMENTABLE IGNORANCE.

On the 27th of April, 1864, there were four hundred and fifty colored soldiers from "Port Hudson" admitted into the Corps d'Afrique general hospital, and, out of the whole number, only fifty of them could tell their proper names and the organizations to which they belonged. Poor fellows! their youth had been spent in the cane-brake and cotton-field, without cultivation, or contact with the active, thinking, and intelligent world around them; and mind in them was almost an utter blank; their whole being seemed merged into passive, dull, and unquestioning obedience and submission to the will and authority of others.

REMARKABLE NAMES.

In looking over the record of the Corps d'Afrique Hospital, any person having a liking for high sounding titles, famous names, and funny soubriquets, can copy at will a notable list. There are now here seventeen George Washingtons, one General Taylor, one General Jackson, three Andrew Jacksons, one John the Baptist, and one Oliver Cromwell. Here also we find Edwin Forrest, Charles Bonnecarrie, John Blazes, Dan Tucker, Thomas

Monday, Tom Sunday, Raphel Raphel, the Prince of Orange, &c., &c. In some instances the negroes are named after the plantation where they are born, and most generally bear the name of their owner.

MARRYING EXTRAORDINARY.

Whenever our armies take possession of slave territory, great numbers of colored people make application to the chaplains of regiments to be married, although many of them have been living together as man and wife for years before. This fact shows that they understand and appreciate the "holy estate" and its responsibilities, and most powerfully reflects on the Christianity, and even civilization, of their former owners. I have had the pleasure to join a large number of them in the relation which is pronounced by the lips of the apostle as "honorable among all men," and which signifies the "mystical union which exists between Christ and his Church."

The signs of the times clearly indicate that this dark stain will be wiped out, and marriage, with all its heaven-sanctioned blessings, will be as sacred among the colored people as it is among the white race.

CHRISTMAS IN NEW ORLEANS.

Christmas day was appropriately observed in all the churches by suitable sermons and other exercises bearing on the glorious advent of the world's Redeemer. In the Catholic churches there were profuse decorations, and the image of the "babe of Bethlehem" was on exhibition, and seemed to be an object of great veneration by the devout of both sexes and all ages. Quite as much interest was manifested in that little wax figure as was possible, almost, if the real person had been before them. I never witnessed such a display of Christmas toys, cakes, confectionery, &c., as was offered here, while the streets and shops were thronged with people. Canal street presented a very lively appearance, being the chief promenade of ladies and gentlemen who could afford to make a gay appearance in their fixing up, and happiness seemed everywhere to prevail.

SABBATH SCHOOL EXHIBITIONS.

On Christmas eve there was a Sabbath School exhibition in the Carondolet St. M. E. Church, which was very tastefully decorated for the occasion. On each side of the platform there was a beautiful Christmas tree, trimmed and loaded with the most tempting fruit, consisting of bon-bons and articles dear to the eye and heart of childhood.

The addresses, recitations, and dialogues of the children were delivered with neatness and remarkable ability, and delighted the crowded audience very much. Great credit is due the managers of this affair, and particularly Mrs. Dr. Newman, to whose skill and tact was due mainly the success of the occasion.

There was a similar celebration held in the Felicity Street Church, and one across the river at Algiers, where I had the pleasure to preside. The speaking surpassed all our expectations, and at the close, our Christmas trees, and other sources, yielded a sumptuous entertainment to teachers and children.

WATCH-NIGHT.

As Methodists, although in a strange land comparatively, we kept up the time-honored custom of watch-meeting, on the last evening of the year, and, while the hosts of our Israel in distant towns and cities, were entering into covenant with the God of Wesley, and our fathers, we met them at the throne of grace, and in two of the principal churches enjoyed a season of refreshing from the presence of the Lord. Some of the members of the Methodist church in this city looked upon this observance as a strange thing, and I suppose are either too sleepy, or too proud, to be found on their knees at midnight on the last day of the old year. New year's day, coming on Sabbath, gave interest to the religious services, and helped to crowd the churches. Calls, and congratulations usual on this day, were deferred until Monday, by the military and state officers, which was right.

A DAY OF JUBILEE.

The 24th of January, 1865, was celebrated in this city as a day of rejoicing, in honor of the edicts of Emancipation passed by conventions, representing the loyal people of Missouri and Tennessee, declaring the freedom of all slaves within their borders, and forever prohibiting slavery or involuntary servitude in those states. At an early hour in the morning, thousands of colored people were seen wending their way toward La Fayette Square. At the residence of the Governor, an immense concourse of soldiers and citizens were assembled, eloquent speakers addressed the multitude, and then a line was formed and the whole concourse paraded through the principal streets of the city. Banners streamed from every available point, music rose in its most soul-stirring strains, and as the procession moved on, cheer after cheer made the welkin ring.

Everybody seemed to be joyful except the poor ex-slave-holders, whose faces were elongated, and their souls became very sad, under the inspiring shouts of freedmen and the prospect to them, of their last hope, the accursed confederacy crumbling to deserved infamy, and ruin. Let the states come on in line, and each one raise upon its highest pinnacle, the emblem of "Liberty throughout all the land, and to all the inhabitants thereof."

THE CHRISTIAN AND SANITARY COMMISSIONS.

The work of the Christian Commission in this department has been very extensive, supplying the soldiers in every camp, barrack, and hospital with good religious literature, and with living teachers of the truth as it is in Jesus. The Sanitary Commission has also performed a noble work among the thousands of soldiers in this department. The "Home" in this city, has proven a great blessing to many a care-worn soldier; for here the detached, discharged, or furloughed, can obtain board and lodging free of charge. This institution is under the jurisdiction of the able and efficient commander of the defenses of the city, General Sherman.

The idea of a Soldiers' Home is, I believe, original with the American people, and is an outgrowth of the exigencies of the war. It is said to have been first instituted in the city of Baltimore in 1861, when troops began to move toward the theatre of war, and many had to be kept stationed there: for it was then a regular hot bed of secession, and furnished incalculable aid and comfort to the rebels, both in men, money, and munitions of war. I am glad to know that loyalty triumphed there, as it will everywhere, by the favor of Almighty God.

These commissions have done such a glorious work, that I cannot helping saying, "God bless every one connected with them in their origin, design, and practical benefits to our brave armies." The history of adventure and achievement connected with their influence will hardly be less wonderful than that of the war itself.

STEAMBOAT COLLISIONS

have for many years furnished the newspapers tales of harrowing horror. Their frequency on the great "father of waters," may in part be accounted for by the fact, that dense fogs are prevalent all along its winding course. I have known the fog to be so heavy, while crossing the ferry, that you could not discern an object five feet from the boat, or at night see the gas lights burning, a short distance from either shore. Our ferry-man informed me that he often lost his reckoning on account of the fog, and failed to make his proper landing on the opposite side of the river. It is no wonder therefore that steamers collide under such circumstances, especially as the hands on board are not celebrated for prudence, but on the contrary, are generally reckless of consequences, and disposed at all times to "let her rip!"

THE CITY AS A MILITARY CAMP,

can be viewed to the best advantage at the time when the field officer of the day takes his rounds to every post, and with a quick scrutinizing eye, ascertains that everything is in good order. Following him you may discover the points where guard-mounting is a regular practice, and the whole city is one great camp, regulated by the strict rules of military order and discipline. This, instead of being a disadvantage, as the secessionists declare, tends to general safety, sobriety, and the free enjoyment of all the rights and privileges of citizenship, and breaking up the terrorism of lawless characters, has purified, and been a blessing to New Orleans.

CHILDREN AND THE CIRCUS.

Major B. Rush Plumley, president of the board of education for the instruction of colored children, having made the necessary arrangements, one day, gratified three thousand, by a visit to "Howe's European Circus," and I understood the sights and scenes they witnessed there produced a tremendous sensation of pleasure. They rolled their optics, and made a display of ivory that was wonderful to behold. Such a pleasure to them was a marked day in their memory, and the considerate Major, I am sure, was amply repaid by the delight he helped to bestow. He is an untiring advocate for the enlightenment of these young minds, and his efforts are being crowned with well deserved success.

A RAID ON THE GAMBLING-HOUSES.

Major-General Hurlbut, the able and efficient commander of the Department of the Gulf, has placed all Christians under obligations to him, for his timely efforts to improve the morals of this city. At the time when the State Legislature was about to confirm the law passed by the late Convention, licensing gambling-houses, this friend of morality had the good sense and courage to issue an order closing all the places of this character, that have so long been a curse and blight to New Orleans. It was also by his order that the theatres were prohibited from having performances on the Sabbath day. All officers and soldiers were also interdicted from visiting whisky shops on the Sabbath. This is a proper exercise of power, and will redound to the credit of the general commanding. It is incalculable what vice, and wretchedness, and crime, such prohibition prevents. Every friend of honesty, temperance, and good order, will approve the act, and admire such soldiers as Generals Hurlbut and Canby, for their efforts to redeem this almost ruined city from dissipation, gambling, and the desecration of the holy Sabbath.

THE EIGHTH OF JANUARY.

The fiftieth anniversary of the Battle of New Orleans happening on the Sabbath, all noisy demonstrations were deferred until Monday, and the Sabbath passed in a manner befitting the stillness and sanctity of the day. Some few, however, supposing it would not do to wait, went off and became intoxicated, and had their accustomed spree.

On Monday morning the slumbering citizens were aroused by the thundering of artillery, fifty guns were fired in honor of the event, by order of the commanding general, and then ensued a general enfilade of small arms, and such a racket as is customary in other localities on the Fourth of July.

Before the rebellion this was an occasion of great enthusiasm, and the annual celebration was participated in by all the citizens who remembered with pride and pleasure the achievements of the immortal Jackson and his brave battalions in their heroic defense of the city, and the defeat of a proud and boasting foe. The value of victory on that day and field, may be estimated by the consequences which would have ensued by the defeat of our army. This city would have fallen, of course, the State of Louisiana and the whole upper valley of the Mississippi would have been captured and conquered, and the war prolonged.

The whole nation, therefore, should keep alive the memory of such a glorious and important event, and be thankful to God that the flag which fifty years ago led our soldiers to the charge, floats to-day triumphantly in the face of treason at home.

May its starry folds ever kindle in the bosom of American patriots an invincible courage to vindicate its honor when tyrants or traitors assail it. And may time in its unnumbered years still perpetuate the spirit of General Jackson and the Republic of our Fathers. May this fair land be the home of the oppressed, an asylum for the poor and down-trodden millions of every land; for Uncle Sam, after all the blood and treasure spent in putting down this rebellion, is still rich enough to give them all a farm!

INAUGURATION DAY.

The fourth of March, 1865, was a high day in this city. At an early hour in the morning, the busy note of preparation gave token that something unusual was on hand, and soon Canal Street became thronged with people, getting into position to witness the scenes about to transpire. Twenty-four fire companies made their appearance, with engines glittering like gold, and bedecked with magnificent wreaths, and a profusion of flags.

The procession was formed by marshals rapidly dashing to and fro, the music fell in and helped to heighten the general interest, and far above and below the "Clay Monument," flags and banners fluttered in the morning-breeze. In compliance with resolutions of general assembly, both houses met at noon to attend the inauguration of Governor Wells, who was to succeed Governor Hahn, he having resigned for the purpose of representing his state in the United States Senate. At the appointed hour, all being in readiness, the proceedings were opened with prayer by the Rev. Dr. Newman, who solemnly invoked the continued aid of Almighty God, to his servant about to be clothed with the high distinction, and weighty responsibilities of governor—that He would grant him ability to discharge successfully the duties involved in his important office, as executor of the will of the people, and endow the representative of the State, with divine direction and blessing, and keep poor mortal ashes from temptation to do wrong.

He also devoutly thanked the Lord of Hosts for victory to the arms of the Union, and the progress of the glorious flag of liberty, and prayed for continued success to the army and navy, to the second term of Abraham Lincoln as president of this great republic, and the nation's standard-bearer, that in his day, and speedily, the banner of an undivided nation might wave, and this iniquitous rebellion might soon be overthrown.

The prayer, which was one of the most appropriate, and eloquent I ever listened to, was followed by patriotic music, and then the oath of office was administered to the new Governor, after which he delivered his inaugural address. The band then played "the star-spangled banner," after which General Hurlbut was introduced to the audience by Ex-Governor Hahn, and was received with great applause. He very eloquently sketched the progress of the war, the baptism of blood and fire through which the country had passed during four years of strife, and alluding to President Lincoln, made some impressive and thrilling encomiums upon that great and good man. He closed with the sentiment: "God preserve the United States, the banner-bearer of freedom."

The band then played "The red, white, and blue," and the ceremonies were closed with the benediction by Dr. Newman, the crowded concourse slowly retired, and this "Inauguration day" will long be remembered in the history of the "Crescent City."

A DISTINGUISHED PATRIOT.

Among the names which will ever be cherished by the country with gratitude for disinterested patriotism, and valuable service during the war, will be that of Dr. J. V. E. Smith, formerly mayor of Boston, and now an agent, and active worker for the Christian Commission in the Department of the Gulf; his head-quarters are at New Orleans. To enter this field he resigned the professorship of Anatomy in the New York Medical College, his sense of duty to his country and her noble defenders being so strong, and his nature so benevolent, he renounced position, ease, and home enjoyments to minister to the wants of the "weary and heavy-laden" among our soldiers, who love him as a father, and confide in him as their best friend. His labors have been arduous, and highly successful in this branch of that great charity, which now commands the wonder and the admiration of all Europe, as well as our own land. So entirely devoted is he to the wants of others that he gives his valuable time, skill, and strength to the cause, without fee or reward, and to my certain knowledge, he has even given the coat off his back to a poor soldier who had none. The Doctor is one of the most intelligent men I have ever known. There is scarcely a place of note on this wide globe he has not visited. His brilliant lectures at the Smithsonian Institute, on his return from extended explorations, commanded the attention of members of Congress, and scientific men everywhere. When the names of our true American heroes are inscribed on the high roll of renown, such men as Professor Smith, will be entitled to a proud place, as a benefactor to his race, and an honor to his country.

CHAPTER XXVII.

OBSERVATIONS CONTINUED.

NEWS OF VICTORY—TIDINGS OF THE ASSASSINATION OF PRESIDENT LINCOLN—JOY TURNED TO MOURNING—GREAT DAY OF HUMILIATION—IMMENSE GATHERING AT LA FAYETTE SQUARE—TEARS AND WOE—MOURNFUL MUSIC—FLAGS AT HALF-MAST—BUILDINGS DRAPED—A CITY FILLED WITH SORROW—PRAYER BY THE REV. DR. NEWMAN—PUBLIC ADDRESSES BY GENERALS HURLBUT AND BANKS—MEETING AT DR. PALMER'S CHURCH—PRAYER BY DR. PEARNE—STIRRING ADDRESSES — CONTRAST — RETRIBUTION FOR SECESH PREACHERS—GREAT SCARE OF THE REBELS—THEIR HOUSES IN SACKCLOTH—REFLECTIONS—THE REPUBLIC STILL LIVES!

BUT a few weeks had run their round, after the occasion just referred to, when alas! the dismal tidings came like a knell to all our anticipations, of the assassination of the honest, patriotic, and liberty-loving President, Abraham Lincoln. Before this awful event was known, news followed news of the victories of Grant around Richmond, the triumphal march of Sherman and his legions, and the climax was reached when it became known as a fact in New Orleans that Lee had surrendered, the Confederacy caved in, and the rebellion at last had its backbone and neck broken! We were almost wild with joy; congratulations flowed on every hand, and people could not sleep, and would not rest, because of the exhilaration produced.

But suddenly these bright sunbeams of gladness are plunged in eclipse, joy is turned to sorrow, and mourning mantles all loyal hearts. The atrocious crime of the 14th of April fell like a dull, heavy stroke upon us, that made us speechless with horror and demented with woe.

The change was so rapid, so unexpected, so tremendous—from the highest pinnacle of our long-looked-for and now realized triumph to the deepest depths of bereavement, as if every man had lost a father, or a first-born, by the cruel stroke of a dagger piercing his heart, that the whole city was quickly robed in mourning and covered with gloom.

The 22d of April was set apart as a day of special mourning, and the history and feelings of that day can never be forgotten. The whole population, it would seem, were moved by one impulse; although some families and individuals doubtless secretly felt a malicious pleasure in the strange and sad event, yet none dare evince the slightest show of triumph. As in northern cities, so here, the temper of a patriot could not brook or bear an insulting word or look from those who were rebels at heart. The public buildings and many private residences were heavily draped in the habiliments of woe. People thronged the streets, wearing badges of mourning. La Fayette Square was again the point to which this now sad and sorrowing mass of humanity wended their way. The fire companies again turned out in full uniform, and their apparatus, as well as themselves, all wearing emblems of the nation's loss. Various societies helped to swell the throng, and solemn music wailed forth its dirge-like strains.

Around the large stand, which was appropriately draped, the multitude gathered, and tears fell like rain. The whole space was crowded with a silent, sad audience. Every banner was fringed with crape, and hung at half-mast, and still the slow, mourning music, helped to make the scene more impressive and awful. Dr. Newman was selected to offer prayer: and such a prayer! pathetic, earnest, soul-moving, while emotion rose like a silent tide, and rolled over that vast throng. The brave and eloquent General Hurlbut then addressed the people, followed by General Banks, whose words never were more wisely chosen, or more effective in making a deep impression.

At the First Presbyterian church a crowd assembled, the building being hung with black. The exercises were commenced with a powerful prayer by the Rev. W. H. Pearne, D.D., followed by an address from Hon. Mr. Roselius, in which he reviewed the administration of our late president, and declared that it had been pure and correct, and that the deluded people of the south had themselves destroyed the institution of slavery. He considered Mr. Lincoln entitled to a degree of veneration second only to the immortal Washington.

Hon. Thomas J. Durant followed, and, in his discourse, said, Liberty had lost one of her firmest friends and noblest defenders in the death of our martyred president. He insisted upon justice being administered to traitors, that there could be *no home in this country for the leaders* of this wicked rebellion, and that Mr. Lincoln's assassination was the result of a preconcerted plan of the rebellious people of the south, who, in their fiendish rage, took this means of revenge.

I wished from my heart that such words as were uttered there that day were burned into the hearts of all the traitors of the land. What a contrast was such a meeting as this to the time when the once infamous, but now repentant Dr. Palmer fulminated his foul treason from the pulpit, Sabbath after Sabbath, and even published his sermons by tens of thousands to fire the heart of the whole southern people with hatred against the government, and bitterness toward the north. No one man, perhaps, did more to influence Louisiana to adopt and practice the heresy of secession than this same Dr. Palmer. Let him now, while he professes to beg pardon of God and man for the errors he taught, and the ruin he helped to bring upon his congregation and countrymen, look forward to the bar of inflexible justice, where he must meet the thousands who were urged to fight and fall as traitors by his counsel. There will be a day of fearful reckoning and terrible retribution for such men, that no bitter tears or whining prayers can alter or avert.

Many of those known to be rebels in this city were the first and most zealous in the work of draping their houses. This was not from sincere feelings of sorrow, but because they wished to deceive union people as to their real sentiments, or because they feared the military.

They fairly trembled with apprehension lest the union soldiery should wreak a summary and indiscriminate vengeance upon them. Indeed there was a rumor among them that all citizens were required by order from army head-quarters to exhibit publicly the emblems of mourning, but such an order was never published or perhaps thought of. The scare, however, did them no harm, but doubtless made many of them reflect seriously, and show a decent respect at least outwardly for the memory of our much-loved President.

God's ways are a great mystery to short-sighted mortals. We cannot penetrate the inscrutable counsels of his will, or understand some of the designs of his dealings. Here faith comes in to aid us, and this faith, while the body of the good and great Abraham Lincoln was borne to its final resting-place, held fast to God, and enabled the nation to bow, and meekly say, "Thy will be done." What a wonder it was, that all through this deplorable period of confusion, the functions of the government were kept regularly in operation, and, instead of falling to pieces by the shock, our God-preserved republic gathered new force and energy from this disaster to carry forward, and accomplish fully its sublime mission.

It was doubtless the hope of those who instigated the conspirators to destroy the lives of the President, Mr. Seward, and others, that there might be a sudden revolution, and in the confusion and excitement of the moment, that the established order of the government might be overthrown—leaving adventurers, who had the nerve and boldness to assume dictatorship, the opening they coveted to reach that position, even through a sea of blood. But God signally foiled their wicked purposes.

Lincoln's name is ever hallowed by its association with martyrdom for principle, and the crown he won and wears will never grow lustreless, while an American heart beats true for liberty.

CHAPTER XXVIII.

OBSERVATIONS CONTINUED.

THE BLACK CODE OF LOUISIANA—KEEP IT BEFORE THE PEOPLE—THE VOICE OF SAGES—CHRISTIAN PATRIOTS—STATESMEN, PHILOSOPHERS AND PHILANTHROPISTS, IN CONDEMNATION OF HUMAN SLAVERY—WHAT THE PEOPLE CAN NOW UNIVERSALLY EXCLAIM — UNION, AND LIBERTY.

To show the friends of freedom, how the South has degenerated and relapsed to Egyptian barbarism, I will present a synoptical view of the pertinently named *Black Code of Louisiana.* Any slave killing or attempting to kill, whether maliciously, or in defense of his family or self, shall be hung. If a slave strike his master or mistress, or their children, or any white overseer, he shall be hung, or be imprisoned at hard labor for ten years. If a slave shoot or stab any person with intent to kill, he shall be hung. If any slave or free person of color shall *attempt* to poison any person, he shall be hung. Any slave guilty of encouraging an insurrection shall be hung. Any slave or free person of color who shall attempt to burn any building or out-house shall be hung. Any slave who shall be guilty for the third offense of striking a white person shall be hung, *unless* the blow was given in defense of his master, some member of his family, or person having charge of him, when the slave shall be *excused*. Any slave forcibly taking goods or money from any person shall be hung, or as the court shall adjudge. Any slave who shall break into a place and attempt to steal, or commit any other crime, shall be hung. Any person cruelly treating a slave shall *not* be fined to exceed two hundred dollars. Any person who shall remove any iron chain or collar fastened to a slave may be imprisoned for six months. If any person shall, by words or action, advise any slave to insurrection, he shall suffer death or imprisonment. Whosoever shall attempt to produce discontent among the free colored or slave population, shall be imprisoned at hard labor, or suffer death. Any person from the bar, the bench, the stage, the pulpit, *or any other place*, who shall be guilty of discourses or signs tending to produce discontent among the free colored, or slave population, or who shall bring into this state any paper, pamphlet or book having such tendency, may be imprisoned twenty-one years, or suffer death. Slaves accused of capital crimes shall be tried by two justices of the peace and ten owners of slaves. Any crime not capital shall be tried by a justice of the peace and *four* owners of slaves. One justice and nine jurors shall constitute a quorum for the trial of slaves accused of capital offenses. If a slave is convicted, the said justice of the peace shall sign the sentence. If the court disagree and do not convict, *it* shall have the power to inflict corporeal punishment according to its pleasure. All slaves sentenced to death or perpetual imprisonment, shall be paid for out of the *public treasury*. A slave may be forced to testify against his fellow-slave, but he is not permitted to testify against a white man. Any slave accused of a capital crime in this parish shall be tried by the judge of the First District Court and six slaveholding jurors. No slave can leave the plantation without a written permission; and any person giving permission without authority shall be fined fifty dollars. Any person who shall mutilate a slave and render him incapable of work, shall be fined fifty dollars, and pay the master two dollars per day for every day lost; and if the slave be forever made unable to work, then the offender shall pay his value, or suffer one year's imprisonment. Any person, having been a slave, returning to this state without permission, shall be forced back to slavery. Any free person of color who may be ordered to leave the state and does not, may be imprisoned at hard labor for five years. Free persons of color are not allowed to land in the state without a legal permit. A master of a vessel must give a bond for the non-landing of free persons of color, &c. &c.

Permit me to ask you to listen to the voice of sages, Christians, patriots, statesmen, philosophers, and philanthropists of this and other nations, concerning this hell-begotten wrong and outrage. Washington said it was his first wish to free America of the curse. Jefferson, the Apostle of Liberty, said he trembled for his country, and declared it was written in the Book of Fate, that the people should be free. Patrick Henry detested slavery with all the earnestness of his nature, and believed the time was not far distant when the lamentable evil would be abolished. Madison denied the right of property in man, and contended that the republican principle was antagonistic to human bondage. Monroe considered slavery as preying upon the very vitals of the Union. John Randolph detested the man who defended slavery. Thomas Randolph deprecated the workings of the evil. Thomas Jefferson Randolph classes the "institution" among the abominations and enormities of savage tribes, and as tending to decrease free populations. Peyton Randolph lamented its existence. Edward Randolph, as member of the Convention that framed the Constitution of our nation, moved to strike out "servitude," and insert "service," because the former was thought to express the condition of slaves, and the latter the obligation of free persons. Henry Clay would never, never, never, by word or thought, by mind or will, aid in subjecting free territory to the everlasting curse of human bondage. The great Benton, in view of the peace and reputation of the white people—the peace of the land—the world's last hope for a free government on the earth, and because it was a wrong, condemned its extension and existence. Colonel Mason contended slavery discouraged the arts and manufactures, made labor disreputable, prevented immigration of whites, who enrich and strengthen a country, produced pernicious effects on manners, made the master a petty tyrant, and invited calamities to the nation. Governor McDowell says this people were born to be free, and their enslavement is in violation of the law of Deity. Judge Iredell, of North Carolina, would rejoice when the entire abolition of slavery took place. William Pinckney, of Maryland, considered it dishonorable and iniquitous. Thomas Marshall, of Virginia, said it was ruinous to the whites. Bolling said the time would come when this degraded and oppressed people would free themselves from their thraldom. Chandler calls it a cancer, and said it would produce commotion and bloody strife. Summers said the evils could not be enumerated. Preston said the slaves were men, and entitled to human rights. Birney, of Kentucky, said the slaveholder had not one atom of right to his slave, and that all people rejoice when they hear that the oppressed are set free. McLane, of Delaware, said, I am an enemy of slavery. Luther Martin, of Maryland, said slavery is inconsistent with the genius of republicanism.

John Jay called it repugnant to every principle of justice and equity. William Jay contended the time had arrived when it was necessary to destroy slavery to save our own liberty. John Quincy Adams—the old man eloquent—said it perverted human reason and tainted the very sources of moral principle. Webster regarded it as a great moral and political evil, sustained by *might* against *right*, and in violation of the spirit of religion, justice and humanity. Noah Webster claimed freedom as the sacred right of every man. De Witt Clinton says the despotisms and slavery of the world would long since have vanished, if the natural equality of mankind had been understood and practiced. General Joseph Warren says personal freedom is the natural right of every man. England, through her Mansfields, calls it odious; her Locke, so vile that a gentleman cannot plead for it; her Pitt, that it should not be permitted for a single hour; her Fox compares it to robbery and murder; her Shakspeare said that heaven will one day free us from this slavery; her Cowper and Miltons have, in immortal verse, execrated it; her Doctor Johnson says no man is, by nature, the property of another; her Doctor Price says, if you can enslave another, he can enslave you; her Blackstone tells us we must transgress unjust human laws, and obey the natural and divine; and her Coke, Hampden, Wilberforce, and many of her other learned and good men, endorsed this doctrine. Ireland's Burke said it ought not to be suffered to exist; her Curran demanded universal emancipation; her great O'Connell, speaking to his countrymen, said he would not recognize them, if they countenanced the horrors of American slavery. Father Mathew said slavery is a sin against God and man, and called loudly on all true Irishmen to help to move on the Car of Freedom. Scotland's voice is as potent in condemnation of this stupendous crime. Her Beattie said it is opposed to virtue and industry, and should be viewed with horror; her Miller said every individual, whatever his country or complexion, is entitled to freedom. France, speaking through her La Fayette, the friend of Washington and Liberty, tells the world he would not have drawn his sword in the cause of America, if he could have conceived that thereby he was founding a land of slavery; his grandson said the abolition of slavery commanded his entire sympathy. Montesquieu said the earth shrank in barrenness from the contaminating sweat of a slave. Louis X. said the Christian religion and nature herself cried out against the state of slavery, and demanded the liberty of all men. Rousseau said slavery and right contradicted and excluded each other. Brissot viewed it as a degradation of human nature. Schiller, Grotius, Goethe, Luther, Humboldt, and thousands of freedom-loving Germans, have spoken deeply in condemnation of this monster iniquity. This noble people were the earliest to denounce the sin, and went so far as to declare the slave justifiable in the murder of his master who refused to let him go free. The greatest of Alexanders has declared, by a solemn ukase, the universal enfranchisement of his people, and sixty millions of human beings are thereby made freemen, to love God and the ways of justice and virtue. Cicero tells us all men are born free, and that law cannot make *wrong right*. Socrates calls slavery a system of outrage and robbery. Plato, that it is a system of the most complete injustice. The great Cyrus said that to fight in order not to be made a slave, is noble. The churches of the world hold this sin as an abomination unto the Lord. The true interpretation of the Bible proclaims liberty throughout all the land, unto all the inhabitants thereof, and commands us to let the oppressed go free, to call no man master, neither to be called masters. Slavery is the black and loathsome sin that will not be forgiven in this world, nor the world to come. Thus the intelligent and great men of all nations denounce this foul system.

Now that the rebellion has gone down, and slavery with it, never to have a resurrection, we as a free and independent people, can universally exclaim :

"Who would sever Freedom's shrine?
Who would draw the invidious line?
Though by birth one spot be mine,
Dear is all the rest.

"Dear to me the South's fair land!
Dear the central mountain band!
Dear New England's rocky strand;
Dear the prairied West!

"By our altars, pure and free!
By the law's deep-rooted tree!
By the Past's dread memory!
By our Washington!

"By our common kindred tongue!
By our hopes, bright, buoyant, young,
By the tie of country strong!
We will still be one!

"Fathers, have ye bled in vain?
Ages, shall ye droop again?
Maker, shall we rashly stain
Blessings sent by Thee?

"No! receive our solemn vow,
While before thy throne we bow,
Ever to maintain, as now,
'Union, Liberty!'"

The great danger is past. The "conflict of ages" is settled. From the reefs, and shoals of political antagonism, the good old Ship of State is saved. Although strained and battered by the "windy storm," she will rapidly right herself for a long and prosperous voyage, and bear to posterity the freight of universal liberty.

It becomes every patriot now, to guard well the heritage God has given us.

"A Union of lakes—a Union of lands,
A Union which none can sever;
A Union of hearts—a Union of hands,
And the flag of our Union forever!"

CHAPTER XXIX.

HOMEWARD BOUND.

OFF FOR CAIRO—THE STEAMER "COMMONWEALTH," SECESH OFFICERS—THE CAPTAIN'S OPINION OF GREEN BACKS—TREATMENT OF A UNION SOLDIER BY THE CLERK—A REBEL LIEUTENANT GETS "TIGHT"—OPINION OF A PASSENGER, AS TO WHERE THE NEW CONSTITUTION OF MISSOURI WAS PREPARED—HIS PREFERENCE FOR EUROPEAN GOVERNMENT—A FEMALE ADVOCATE FOR POOR JEFF—ABANDONED PLANTATIONS—PORT HUDSON—BATON ROUGE—NATCHEZ—REAL CHARACTER OF A PROFESSED UNION MAN—VICKSBURG—THE GREAT SIEGE AND CAPTURE—GENERAL DAVIDSON—ELECTION—REBELS IN THE ASCENDANT—MARTIAL LAW STILL NECESSARY—LAKE PROVIDENCE—THE FOURTH JULY ON BOARD—NAPOLEON—MEMPHIS—INCIDENTS—SCENERY—WASTE LANDS—A DROWNED MAN—ARRIVAL AT CAIRO—HOME AGAIN.

I LEFT New Orleans on the 1st of July, 1865, on leave of absence, to visit my friends in Pennsylvania, and supposed, when I stepped on board the steamer "Commonwealth," bound up the Mississippi, that I should have to return at the expiration of my furlough. Circumstances, however, so altered the case, that my departure was for an indefinite period, and my farewell to the scenes and associations of the "Crescent City," was perhaps, for ever.

The "Commonwealth" was a first-class river-steamer,

with ample accommodations for a large passenger list, and a pleasant sojourn during the progress of the upward trip. Her officers, I found to be reserved on the subject of outspoken and hearty adhesion to the government. Although they rated themselves as Union men, yet I more than suspect, the majority of them were among the disappointed chivalry, who mourn over the misfortunes of the bursted bubble of southern confederacy, and need a severe and thorough "reconstruction."

It is, indeed, a notorious fact that most of the officers of the river steamers, all through the war, have been downright rebels; and many of them have come to grief in consequence of their sympathy with treason. They have been afforded many opportunities for meditation and amendment in various guard houses and prisons, under the eye of some of Uncle Sam's boys, with fixed bayonets, and a grim determination to "settle their hash" without extraordinary provocation, should they show a disposition to be unruly.

The captain of our noble steamer entertains no very favorable opinion of "greenbacks." He says, like the Jews, they have no redeemer! yet he much prefers, and doubtless has for some time past, to receive this kind of currency to the scrip of his favorite party in the south, when taking an equivalent for passage or freight. The clerk of the boat appeared to be a little in advance of the others in sentiment, and evinced his hatred to our cause by inhuman treatment of a poor Union soldier on board.

I felt it to be my duty to interfere in the premises, and, but for this, it would have gone very hard with the veteran in the hands of such cruel and unprincipled rascals as these river rebels have shown themselves to be.

There were quite a large number of passengers on board, most of whom were, or professed to be, of the straight-out, unterrified, and not-to-be-conquered class of secessionists. They made their conversation studiously disagreeable and insulting to the friends and flag of this glorious union. A rebel lieutenant among them seemed to be a special favorite with both the officers and passengers, and was pressed so earnestly and often to "take something," that he soon became as drunk and as silly as a fool, and acted accordingly. A man of sense and patriotic impulses, in such a crowd, must bear a vast amount of insult and impudence, especially from these swaggering "Johnny Rebs," who, on the strength of bad whisky, fight their battles over again, and immortalize themselves by the tales they repeat of personal bravery in killing Yankees.

The conversation turning on the Missouri constitution, an old dilapidated individual declared that, in his opinion, that document emanated from Massachusetts, and was dictated and written somewhere in the meridian of Boston. He said he liked the laws of Europe better than those of this country, because there the poor man was not allowed to vote. I thought, at the time, what a great blessing it would be if all these old broken-down dignitaries of the aristocratic dynasty that has, thank

God, been broken up, would leave this country. It would certainly be for the country's good if they would emigrate to the regions of despotism, and end their days in the worship of peerage and tinseled royalty.

I heard some of these rebels talk over their plans to embarrass the government at every point, and aid those who had been in armed rebellion in their efforts to gain power and position in the administration of public affairs. A secesh female was very earnest in argument with a gentleman of union sentiments, showing the virtues of Jeff. Davis, and his claims to the love and sympathy of the people. The other, however, put an extinguisher on the question by saying he ought to be hung.

In passing up the Mississippi the traveler will see a great many abandoned plantations on every hand. Our pilot thinks they can never be cultivated with success unless slavery be continued, but we differ with him on that point, and time will soon demonstrate the fact that he and thousands like him are under a great mistake.

Port Hudson, La., comes into view, and reminds us of General Banks and his forces who lay so long in close proximity to this little town. It is situated on the east bank of the river, and appears to be a place of but little importance, aside from the part it played in the history of the war.

Next appears Baton Rouge, once the capital of the state, and the scene of some severe fighting. Natchez is quite a large and imposing town, standing on a bold bluff on the east bank. A certain man resides there, whom the government has confided in, and protected, as a staunch friend of the Union; but when his son who had been in the rebel army returned home, after surrendering as a prisoner of war, this supposed Union-loving father shut the door in his face because he had disgraced himself by a surrender to the Yankees! This is not the first instance, by a long way, in which rebels have hoodwinked our officers by deception and false pretense.

Vicksburg, Mississippi, soon comes into notice. This place is memorable, as offering such a long and stubborn resistance to General Grant, who finally captured it and took possession on July 4th, 1863. It is a city of about eight thousand inhabitants, and is four hundred miles above New Orleans. It is now under guard by a force of fifteen hundred colored troops, with General Davidson as commander of the post. I heard a couple of the citizens invite this officer up to drink with them, and he refused to do so, which fact raised him considerably in my estimation. There had been an election held here on July 1st, in which the rebels, as in all other places, under the present policy of reconstruction succeeded in electing candidates of the most ultra Southern stripe. Governor Sharkey's private secretary, I am told, is an ex-rebel colonel, which, however well such an arrangement may suit the views of the people, is an insult to loyalty. The South is highly pleased with the present attitude of the general government, and most agreeably disappointed in the measures of leniency pursued towards some of her most criminal and dangerous citizens. They have everything their own way in many places, and are as insolent and overbearing as ever. Give them the reins again, and Union-loving people must flee for their lives. Let them manage their own affairs, and liberty, law, and everything for which our brave armies fought, is as much a dead letter as if they, and not us, were the conquerors. If order and peace is to be restored, and life and property protected, if the colored man is indeed a freeman, and his friends are to have liberty of speech, nothing will answer yet awhile but strong military occupation, and the steady hand of martial law, until these traitors are thoroughly subjugated and safely reconstructed.

Leaving Vicksburg, our course was still up the river, when the morning of the glorious Fourth dawned upon us. The day passed, I am ashamed to say, without the least demonstration on board our floating palace, to signify the joy of American citizens, not only in memory of the Declaration of Independence, but in celebration of our victory over the combinations of internal treason, and the overthrow of the bogus Confederacy. While cannon are thundering, bonfires blazing, and the hearts of millions in the great North and West throbbing with emotions of thankfulness to our fathers' God, here we are cabined and confined among a set of sulky passengers, who it seems would rather curse than bless the starry flag that waves in triumph elsewhere to-day. Even the flag is not hoisted on our boat, which shows beyond all question that the captain is a rebel.

When I say there was no demonstration on board, I ought perhaps to make an exception in favor of the American citizens of African descent, who got up a rousing dance on the lower deck, and enjoyed themselves in their own peculiar style, without let or hindrance.

I noticed, as we passed, a place called Lake Providence, but there is nothing of importance about the place, except a steamboat landing. Successively, we passed Napoleon, Arkansas; White River, Friar's Point, Mississippi; and Helena, and reached the City of Memphis, which is on the Tennessee side on a high bluff, and occupies the most notable and commanding site for a city, between Cairo and the Belize. Memphis contained a population of over forty thousand before the rebellion. The war was damaging to its business interests to a very large extent, but trade is reviving, and things begin to assume a lively appearance about the streets and landing again. The city is very attractive to a stranger, who will find here many evidences of taste, enterprise, and refinement. Fort Pinckney commands both the city and river front, with its rows of heavy guns. "Court Square," in the centre of the city, is a very beautiful place.

Fort Pillow may be seen on the east bank as you pass, and is memorable as the scene of a diabolical massacre of Union soldiers and citizens, including even women and children by the blood-thirsty vagabonds who composed Forrest's marauding band. The very name will, in all future time be a standing rebuke to the wicked men, who let loose such demons on a defenseless few, and murdered them in cold blood. Surely a just God will remember such wicked acts, and not allow the guilty to live and die unpunished.

New Madrid is on the Missouri side of the river, and appears to some advantage. Hickman is next reached, and there is but little left of it, after the numerous raids that were made by parties, whose delight seemed to be destruction, and whose track was everywhere marked by devastation and ruin. Columbus comes into view, and is, as will be remembered, the highest point on the river where the rebels attempted to fortify themselves, and withstand the onset of our armies. Large portions of the country all the way up from New Orleans, are low, and constantly liable to inundations; the scenery is very monotonous, presenting few features of attraction to the eye of a traveler.

There are millions of acres of unoccupied land all along the banks of the Mississippi, which, doubtless, in the course of time, will be reclaimed and put in a state of cultivation. But population must increase, and immigration turn its mighty tide in this direction; then improvement will begin, and the great valley, capable itself of supporting one hundred millions of people, will become the very heart of our immense country.

On the 6th of July, as we were rapidly steaming against the current, an object was observed floating on the surface of the river, which, as it swept past, proved to be the body of a drowned man. This sight awakened some peculiar and sad reflections in my mind. Who was he? Where and how did the life, so dear to him, and perhaps so valuable to friends or family, suddenly close? and whither drifting, without a coffin, a tear, or the rites of Christian burial?

My destination was Cairo, Ill., which was reached in due time, and going on shore, I enjoyed an opportunity of giving this celebrated place, which figured so prominently in connection with military operations conducted by the great western wing of the Union army, a thorough personal examination. It is located at the junction of the Ohio and Mississippi Rivers, and covers the point of land which lies between both. It is now a large, populous, and flourishing town, having improved greatly since the commencement of the war. The chief drawback to its prosperity arises from the constant danger there is, when the rivers rise, to be overflowed. Levees and embankments protect it ordinarily, and the citizens, to be provided against emergencies, have constructed sidewalks at an elevation of ten to fifteen feet above the surface of the ground, on which they may travel to and fro in times of high water, and enter their dwellings through the second or third story window. It is said that this is quite an unhealthy locality, but men will brave health for the sake of wealth, and go through fire as well as flood to accomplish the purposes of their worldly ambition. The locality, if the ground were higher, would suit admirably for a very large and enterprising city.

My next mode of transit was by rail to Indianapolis, thence to Pittsburg, and on to Philadelphia, where I arrived safely on the 8th of July, making the entire trip from New Orleans in eight days. I need not here detail the incidents of my rapid railroad journey, and could not, if even I tried, describe the feelings with which I once more entered the city of Brotherly Love. Approaching it, the very spires and domes, its uniform blocks of brick and mortar, and regular streets and squares, and, more than all, its people, among whom I claim many cherished friends, gave me indescribable joy.

CONCLUSION.

CHAPTER XXX.

CONCLUSION.

MUSTERED OUT—REVIEW OF FOUR YEARS—OBSERVATIONS ON THE PROSECUTION OF THE WAR—DESPERATION OF THE ENEMY—NECK OR NOTHING—ABSURDITY OF THE MILK-AND-WATER POLICY—MEANNESS OF NORTHERN ALLIES OF JEFF. DAVIS—THE CONSTITUTION—SELF-PRESERVATION—TRAITORS SHOULD BE PUNISHED—COMING EVENTS—THE SOUTH A SPOILED CHILD—RECONSTRUCTION—THE PISTOL AND BOWIE KNIFE POLICY—CHARACTER OF THE MEN WHO FOUGHT THE FIGHT—BRAVERY AND ENDURANCE—A JUST CAUSE—FAITH IN GOD—OVERTHROW OF SLAVERY, THE FUTURE OF THE COLORED RACE—SOUTHERN HATRED—OPPRESSION—SWORN ENEMIES SHOULD NOT BE ALLOWED TO CONTROL THE COUNTRY—EQUALITY TO ALL—NO DANGER OF COLLISION—THE NATION'S NEEDS—A GENERAL REVIVAL OF RELIGION—THE TRUE BOND OF UNION—LESSONS OF THE WAR.

WITH the obligation resting upon me to return to New Orleans, and report myself for duty within a specified time, I was hurrying through a round of very pleasant visits, to places, and persons associated with my earlier life, and making preparations for my departure, when, on the 25th of August, 1865, a document found its way to my temporary address, the contents of which gave me the highest degree of satisfaction. The rapid reduction of the army, the breaking up of hospitals, and the consequent duty of mustering out of service, a large proportion of post and army Chaplains, brought me the welcome relief of an honorable discharge from farther service in the relation I had sustained. Not that such service was disagreeable, or that I had become weary in my work, for I did not intend to back out of responsibility so long as in the judgment of others I was needed: but it was natural to suppose, had I returned, it would have only involved a tedious journey there, and in a short time, home again for good. My papers, therefore, came at a most opportune moment, and in a very brief period of correspondence with the Department, I had the gratification to feel that my accounts were all settled, and my record approved in an honorable and satisfactory manner.

It remained, therefore, for me to turn my attention to the demands of duty in civil life, and again fall in line with my brethren and fellow-laborers, of the Philadelphia Conference, as a worker in the ranks of the regular itinerancy.

In giving the foregoing chapters a hasty review, I find but few subjects falling within the scope of my title page, that have not been touched upon, and however brief, or incidental the allusion, yet my views have been stated and observations given, with frankness, emphasis, and a strict regard to unvarnished fact.

As I look back over the record of four fleeting years, and try to compass in my thoughts the wonderful story of war, with its marshaled millions, its fierce encounters, its rapid evolutions, its sad, and yet thrillingly grand results, I suppose I am not alone when I confess, that the whole drama, upon which the curtain has now fallen, is more like a dream than the reality.

The historian who shall faithfully write this record, will not lack for evidence of the great truth, that there is a "God in history;" that "his ways are not our ways, neither are his thoughts our thoughts." He sets his bounds, appoints his own times, modes, and seasons for mighty revolutions; and then, as though perfectly natural causes, conspired to render certain results inevitable, He, the Almighty Ruler, works out the counsels of his will, whoever and whatever may oppose.

Look at Israel in the land of groaning! Look at tribes, and peoples down the roll of past centuries, crying, O Lord! how long? Look at men professing to be wise, planning, predicting, and foreshadowing this, that, or the other event, as contingent on their theories of government, morals, or philosophy: but "He that sitteth in the heavens, shall laugh: the Lord shall have them in derision!"

"Blind unbelief is sure to err,
And scan his work in vain;
God is his own interpreter,
And he will make it plain."

Who does not now see plainly that this nation needed a chastisement of just such a character and in just such proportion as it has received for its complicity with the "sum of all villanies;" its subserviency to proud, wicked men, and its time-serving and truckling policies for party power and the lust of office, of wealth, and of godless ambition!

It was written of old, "He will not forget the cry of the needy," and, "although hand join in hand, the wicked shall not go unpunished." Behold the fulfilment! Truth, long crushed to earth, comes forth in its native proportions of beauty; righteousness, trodden under foot, asserts its sway; and now a redeemed nation should humbly adore the providence, the power, and the mercy that has saved it from shipwreck and final destruction.

From stage to stage of development we have been led on successively until ideas once spurned as crude, unreasonable, or insane, are adopted; and education goes on year after year of bloody war, until seeming impossibilities become the recognized doctrines and practical outgrowths of the exigencies of these tremendous years of civil strife. The "considerate judgment of mankind," to which the great Lincoln appealed in closing that immortal proclamation which unfettered millions of bondmen, after appalling wonder and reluctant assent, slowly, but surely and soundly, comes round, with its confirmatory sanction, its calm endorsement, and, finally, its unmeasured applause; until the world is resounding with the pæans of liberty to all, victory for right, and the principle of free government and republican liberty vindicated, settled, and established on the American continent forever!

"From this time," therefore, "it shall be said, 'What hath *God* wrought?'" For "God" hath gained for his own eternal name the glory and strength, the wisdom and might, the honor and everlasting praise. Infidelity has waned before the nation's growing faith, and men who refer events to accident or chance, have learned, in the school of rigid trial, a better and more consistent philosophy.

It is useless now to speculate as to what might or might not have been the consequences of this or that cause. As surely as Pharaoh's eyes were blinded, and his heart allowed to grow more and more implacable, so surely did that Being who presides over the destinies of nations, and in whose hands are the hearts of all men, allow the leaders of the great rebellion to become infatuated with their folly, and insane as to the end of their mad revolt. The mustering of armies, the furore, the fiery zeal, and the reckless desperation of the enemy, growing more vicious in the flush of apparent success, and more callous in the midst of disaster and defeat, all combined to make the final catastrophe to their arms, their flag, their boasted prowess, resources, and the staple of their sunny clime; and to the corner-stone and pillar of their Confederacy, more signal and irreparable.

Abolitionists wrote, reasoned, and often raved, against the institution of slavery: philanthropists perilled life, in the endeavor to scatter a little light, where darkness, bitterness, and cruelty reigned; Christians prayed and waited, and lo! after all, the abettors, the advocates, and the actual owners of "personal property" in flesh and bones, and blood, themselves strike the blow, that rebounds and breaks the manacles from shrivelled hands, almost paralyzed with long "stretching forth unto the Lord of Sabaoth."

Slaveholders become their own executioners, and blindly, like Samson, pull down the temple, they had reared, in crashing ruin on their own heads. The boom of that gun pointed at the "Star of the West," standing in toward Sumter one day, rolls on, reverberating as the knell, the death-knell of American slavery. Its tones struck terror to southern hearts, and this is why their cause became a "neck or nothing" affair. From the start it was their motto to "rule, or ruin," and the wonder now is that our government failed so long to comprehend the situation, and leaned toward mercy, compromise, and milk-and-water policy, until its own honor and very life, had well nigh gone down, in the black, seething whirlpool of domestic insurrection.

We can recall the facts of 1861, when statesmen could with impunity extol Jeff Davis, and newspapers assail the powers that be; when our enemies in the North joined hands with our desperate foes to subvert civil liberty, and all the vulgar epithets in the dictionary, were marshalled and used against the man whose honest heart welled out in "Charity toward all, and malice toward none;" when caricatures, inuendoes, and malicious slanders were used to inflame the rabble, and bring the bloody tide of war to all portions of the noble north! And now, these mean, unprincipled, and, as yet unhung, incendiaries in the north, step forward like Betsy's poltroon of a husband, in the story, to claim their share of credit in killing the bear! Only a few days ago, one of these sham bedlamite enemies actually declared that it was *his* party and its principles that saved the nation, and suppressed the rebellion! O shame! where is thy blush?

It was a favorite, and very popular rallying-cry with these detestable traitors in the rear, to say the "Constitution" had been violated, the safeguards of Liberty destroyed, and under the beneficent working of a suspension of the habeas corpus, they felt insecure and very unhappy.

No doubt of it. "No rogue e'er felt the halter draw with good opinion of the law." So with them. Loyal men were not in mortal trepidation, did not rail against martial law, or feel their hearts thump, at every knock at their doors. *They* could sleep at nights, and go about their business with a clear conscience. They knew moreover, that this hue and cry about the "Constitution" was all "clap trap." In no single article, section, paragraph or line, had that glorious instrument been overleaped. Does it not expressly provide for emergencies? Does it not specify the duty of the executive, in times of insurrection? Does it not make his duties imperative, under a solemn oath? Has it not inherently the principle and the power of self-preservation? And does it not afford authority to hang traitors? Ah! there's the rub. Carry out the Constitution and you may depend on it, the price of hemp will take an upward tendency; for there are thousands who are fit for nothing, in all candor and earnestness, but to execute a modern hornpipe with their toes above the surface!

The hangman has, however, been often cheated of his due, and in all probability many, if not most of these flagrant offenders will, true to the wriggling and slippery propensities of their namesake, escape the just reward of their deeds.

What concerns the future of this country now is the great question, "Who shall rule?" "Coming events," it is said, "cast their shadows before," and the indications are growing fearfully significant and strong that the animus of treason is not quite extinct. Like the old field adder, a little warmth of public patronage or political power, will restore their poisonous propensities North and South, and soon we shall have all the knavery of corrupt principles permeating our national councils, if the enemies of our country are not kept under.

The South, like a spoiled child, has been petted with government pap so long, and indulged in its fits of bad humor, during which it has upset and broken things generally, to such an extent that its old proclivity is returning as though nothing had happened, and about the very halls of the White House and the doors of Congress, hungry tribes of ex-generals—colonels—captains and heads of *headless* departments have the brazen effrontery to congregate; no longer it is true, with pistol and bowie-knife blustering for their rights, but whining for something in the way of position and power.

I suppose most of these fallen heroes, if they can't command a seat in the Senate, or a place in the Cabinet, or even a few thousand a year in some subordinate office where there is nothing to do but chew tobacco, would come down, like the office-hunter in General Jackson's day, to accept thankfully an old pair of breeches!

Seriously, the best method of "reconstruction," and the safest for posterity and future peace, is to allow no man or set of men who have taken part in the murder of Union soldiers or citizens, and who premeditated the murder of the nation itself, to hold any office whatever. Let good, honest Union men who have a clean record be sent into all the Southern Territory, and back them up with the irrepressible bayonet, at whatever expense to the national exchequer, and let the laws be administered by those who are reliable, and not by vagabonds who have proved themselves to be recreant to every obligation, faithless to every trust, and whose "reconstruction" to be valid, should be like the little boy's old knife which needed new blades, new spring, and a bran new buck-horn handle! It is folly to play with fire. It is absurd to expect honor and fidelity where both have been outraged. A perusal of the daily papers will convince any unprejudiced mind that there is a great deal of work in the way of subjugation yet to be done, and a great deal of wisdom and firmness needed to do it.

As a measure of sheer justice, as well as national safety, the men to colonize, control, and revolutionize the old ideas and order of things in the late rebel states, are those who fought the fight and, under God, saved the country.

Some will say they are unfit for such responsibilities. Why so? Who are they? With some exceptions, that have been easily detected, the great majority of our officers, yea, and multitudes of the steady, patriotic soldiers, are men of the finest education, genteel in manners, refined in character, liberal in their views, and well versed in the science of government. Those who suppose our officers and men were mere adventurers have not witnessed what I have seen. In the camp, on the march, in battle, or maimed with wounds in the hospital, these brave men were true as steel. Not a murmur from their lips, even under the knife, or a sigh of regret while pining in loneliness. And why? Because the cause in which they embarked was, to their inmost souls' consciousness, a just one. Because they had firm reliance on God, and believed the great issue was in his hands, and would be successful.

These men understand the posture of affairs. They fought to reëstablish the national authority, and plant again the flag in every spot where the one had been defied, and the other insulted and spit upon. And more than this. They have discrimination enough to know the cause, and reprobate the occasion of resistance against a benign government. They pressed their energies toward the extirpation of that cause. For the overthrow of slavery they endured the toil and braved the danger which met them at every turn. And they mean that this business shall be a finality. Slavery in any form, oppression in every respect, and the avarice that wrings out of the sweat of the poor, defenseless, and unlettered African the means for pampered idleness, they are determined shall never lift its hydra-head again.

In the hands of good, true, untainted loyal men, alone, the poor negro is safe from indignity, imposture, and continued degradation. Leave the freedmen to the tender mercies of their former owners as neighbors, and they shall be hunted like sheep, and ground under the heel of a hatred that has lately become intensified to fury.

The future of the colored race in this land is one of the problems over which hangs a thick vail of obscurity. Shall the prophets who have declared their extermination, or the politicians who have sneered at their efforts to become intelligent and useful citizens, or the demagogues who catch the ague every time political equality is mentioned—shall these have things all their own way? God forbid!

He that hath so strangely opened up for this long-neglected people a path through the deep waters, will feed them in their present wilderness state, and spread his covering wings around their unprotected heads; and in due time we shall see a silver lining fringe the gloomy cloud, and a future for this race which will be characterized by independence, consideration, and respect, and advancement to that inheritance to which the fathers of this nation declared all men to be born.

The Declaration of Independence and the Emancipation Proclamation must now be framed together. The great fact announced in the former becomes a practical thing in the latter, and is now the supreme law of this "heaven-favored land," although it required four-score years of schooling to bring the popular conscience and heart squarely up to its avowal and maintenance.

Southern hatred must be put under bonds for decent behaviour. Oppression must cease, and the sworn enemies of our nation must be educated into proper subjection by the "logic of events," and the strong and steady hand of centralized power.

Instead of becoming our rulers these late rebels must accept the "issue of battle," and in a generation or two, perhaps, their descendants may become eligible to public confidence and a share in the government.

In the doctrine of human equality before the law, and on this position I take my stand, there appears to me to be nothing like danger to liberty or disaster to the internal harmony and peace of the community. There can be no collision of races unless it is provoked by the white people. It is reduced to an absolute certainty that the educated colored man, if let alone, will not meddle with us. Treat him fairly and he will appreciate your kindness. Pay him for his labor and he will earn faithfully his bread and butter. Let him vote—ah! here's the trouble—and he *won't* vote for old hunkers; he won't forget who the *copperheads* were; he will tell his children and his children's children to beware of a party that rose to power and long maintained supremacy solely on oppression of the colored race; and to its last gasp, tried to rivet the chains on that people with merciless vigor and unabated cruelty.

Well—the world moves! What a transition in five years? What a triumph of principle over self-interest, pride, and sectional bitterness, we can rejoice in to-day? The black man is a freeman, at least in form. The white man who wanted liberty of opinion, of speech, and of the press, is free. The Bible is unfettered and the gospel is free! Hallelujah!

No longer can "Mason and Dixon's line" bound the spread of liberal sentiments, popular education, or the fifty-eighth chapter of Isaiah! We have now a fair field, and may God prosper the right.

Before the calamity of war overspread the land with darkness and wailing, there came an unseen hand, a silent, but powerful force of conviction, which touched the hearts, and tendered the feelings of tens of thousands, leading them to prayer, repentance, and trust in Christ, as the all-sufficient and only Saviour. We recall the great revival of 1858, and its incidents of thrilling power, and gracious visitation of the Holy Spirit. What does this whole nation need most at present?

One will say "a chief magistrate, who understands his responsibility, and will do right." Another will look to the Congress of the nation, and say, "Here is the centre and source of our strength and safety."

Others will give opinions as diverse as their own varying views, on "reconstruction," tariffs, taxes, and commercial, or industrial interests. But this whole country needs, now, more than anything else, in my judgment, a wide-spread, deep, and powerful revival of the work of God. This alone can make crooked paths straight, and rugged places, in every department, even. This alone, can furnish an enduring basis, and effectual bond of fraternity between enemies and friends.

This will heal the breach, restore the waste places, and bring forth in the desert land springs of water, and the bloom of prosperity again. A thorough revival, in which God's people shall be quickened to holy zeal, and sinners by hundreds of thousands, converted from the error of their ways, will right up the gallant ship that was so nearly stranded, and fill the hamlets and homes of the nation, where mourning has been endured for a weary night, with joy and rejoicing.

For a revival then let Christ's ambassadors preach, and all his people pray, until the little cloud appearing, shall spread over all the sky, and teeming showers of blessing come on the thirsty land. Then shall there be a sound in the tops of the mulberry-trees, and the God whose goodness we have all seen and acknowledged, will be honored and glorified, and He will return unto us, and cause his face to shine, and we shall be saved.

It is coming! The drops are falling! Sinners are

crying! Saints are full of immortal hope! The churches in this city, and elsewhere,—O may it be so everywhere! are waking up to effort, and the prospect is that even as in former times, and much more abundantly, our Father in heaven will remember Zion, and turn the hearts of the disobedient to the wisdom of the just.

The lessons of the war will be lost on us unless we are brought nigh to the throne: unless the whole nation is humbled on account of sin, and then exalted on account of practical righteousness. "Help, Lord!" "It is time for Thee to work!" And for us, a people preserved to Thy praise, "It is high time to awake out of sleep."

As I lay down my weary pen, and commit these pages to the press, I am happy to assure the reader, that in preaching salvation to perishing souls, and pointing the inquirer to the Lamb of God, I hope to spend the remnant of my days. Pray, that my faith may fail not, and that we may meet at last on the banks of eternal deliverance!

THE END.

www.ingramcontent.com/pod-product-compliance
Lightning Source LLC
LaVergne TN
LVHW010229110826
845151LV00004B/1234

* 9 7 8 1 4 2 5 5 2 5 8 9 7 *